THE LOST GENERATION

To Nannette Roberson
May God be with you
today and forever.

Kymo Dockett

January 26, 2006

THE LOST GENERATION

Why They Don't Serve God?

by

Kymo Dockett

Aventine Press

Copyright 2005, Kymo Dockett
First Edition

Without limiting the rights under copyright reserved above, no part of this publication may be reproduced, stored in or introduced into a retrieval system, or transmitted, in any form or by any means (electronic, mechanical, photocopying, recording, or otherwise), without the prior written permission of both the copyright owner and the publisher of this book.

Published by Aventine Press
1023 4th Ave #204
San Diego CA, 92101
www.aventinepress.com

ISBN: 1-59330-341-6

Printed in the United States of America

ALL RIGHTS RESERVED

Dedication

This book is dedicated to my father and mother, Richard and Wilma Dockett. Thank you for being great role models to me. I also want to dedicate this book to my twin brother, Kymal, my sister, Pamela, and the greatest nephew in the world, Octavian Dockett. To my friends, Jeffrey Banks, Eva Nolen, Latisha Grady, the Kellums, Lloyd Wharton and the Journeymen, thank you for being there for me over the years. And lastly, I can't neglect my *What's The Word* family.

Table of Contents

Introduction..1
Chapter 1   A Historical Look....................................3
Chapter 2   Ten Myths about Christianity..............19
Chapter 3   The Hip-Hop Generation......................33
Chapter 4   Reaching the Hip-Hop Culture............41
Chapter 5   Christian Hip-Hop 101..........................51
Chapter 6   Action Plan..59
Bonus Section #1:   The History of Christian
     Hip-Hop..63
Bonus Section #2:   What Awards: Honoring the
     Best of 2005...77
Bonus Section #3:   Top Ten Greatest
     Christian Hip-Hop Albums.............................81
Bonus Section #4:   Q&A Session on
     Christian Hip-Hop..85
References And Notes...96

Introduction

"The Church is the one institution that exists for those outside it."
- William Tyndale

I wrote this book to answer the following question: Why do so few members of this generation (the hip-hop generation) serve God? According to the Barna Research Group, only three out of 10 people in their 20s in this country (31 percent) attend church in a typical week, compared to four out of 10 of those in their 30s (42 percent) and nearly half of all adults in their 40s (49 percent). If these trends continue, America can expect only about 20 percent of the next generation to attend church. Why are we seeing numbers that suggest that the church is losing its relevance in this country? We are about to uncover the answers to this mystery.

I was once one of those individuals whose church attendance was lacking. I am a 32-year-old male who gave my heart to Christ when I was 20 years old. After more than a decade of attending church, I got tired of going. Throughout this period, I still loved and faithfully served God, as I continued to operate a Christian magazine and write this book.

Nevertheless, I looked up one day and realized that I had not been to church in more than a year. I personally got tired of its humdrum routine; it was not impacting my life, and I was weary of being a part of something that was not changing the world for Christ.

There are millions of people between the ages of 20 and 40 who have their own unique accounts of why they don't attend church. At some point, the church needs to start listening to these young adults, before they lose a whole generation.

We live in different times. Years ago, if you told someone you went to church, that meant something. Now, in this generation's eyes, it means absolutely nothing. This is a generation that has turned its back on God and has little or no respect for the house of God.

There are many young adults who would rather seek comfort in a bottle of liquor or in illegal drugs than go to church for help. There are others who would prefer to call on someone like Dionne Warwick, or an individual just as confused as they are, rather than obtain advice from a church leader. This is especially true for men; millions of them pack into bars and football stadiums on a Sunday morning, but very few think about going to church. But is it possible to change these and other, similar trends?

Anyone who studies history will see that our nation has not always been this way. The church was once the foundation of the Black community. People looked to the church for leadership and for help in times of crisis. It was also a place to develop intimate relationships. Now, some communities don't even want churches in their neighborhoods. What has the church become today, and what will become of the church in the future? These are just a couple of questions I will examine in the course of this book. I believe that there are plenty of solutions to this epidemic.

My book is for those who are tired of looking around in churches across this country and seeing so few young people. This book is for those who are looking for something real from God, and who are tired of going through the motions as a Christian. Lastly, this book is for all of those who want to reach the hip-hop generation, a generation that will be lost by the church if we do not discover the reason why the members of that generation do not serve God.

Chapter 1

A Historical Look

"If you read history, you will find out that the Christians who did most for the present world were precisely those who thought most of the next."
                                                                    - C. S. Lewis

Throughout this book, why the hip-hop generation attends church at such a low rate is a question we will examine from different perspectives. We begin with a historical standpoint. In this chapter, I compare and contrast various other generations with the hip-hop generation, and use this as the basis for offering seven reasons why church has become so much less popular among the young adults of today.

For the purposes of this discussion, "generation" is defined not only by the period of time during which a group was born, but also by the accomplishments of that particular group. For example, we identify people born between 1927 and 1945 as belonging to the civil rights generation. Why are they labeled in this way? This is the group of people who helped African-Americans gain their civil rights. I will be referring to five major generations in this chapter. Here is a brief summary of those groups.

Post-Slavery Generation

The first generation to which I will refer is the post-slavery generation. Its members were born between 1865 and 1926. This particular group was the first generation that had the opportunity to set up communities and build a solid foundation for free African-Americans in this country. They helped African-Americans to successfully transition from slavery and migrate across the country. Organizations like the National Urban League helped this group find jobs and housing, and adjust to urban life. Racist organizations (like the Ku Klux Klan) and unfair laws often stood in their way.

During this period, African-Americans began to form Christian associations. The largest was the group of Black Baptist churches that formed after a schism in 1915 at the National Baptist Convention. Blacks ended up re-creating Christianity for themselves, mixing African rituals and practices with the language and rites of European Christianity, Holy Scripture and the music of revivals. This re-creation began during slavery, as Blacks were offered opportunities by white Christian missionaries to create and conduct their own meetings, to become literate, and to build their own communities.

Civil Rights Generation

Post-slavery's spiritual legacy and struggle for equality carried into the civil rights generation. The civil rights generation represented a group of people who were born from 1927 to 1945. They used civil disobedience techniques to gain civil rights for African-Americans. The Bible inspired many of the methods they utilized, as African-Americans attempted to remain devoted to God and fight for equality at the same time. Organizations like the Southern Christian Leadership Conference (1954-1970) developed the framework of this movement.

The church spearheaded most of the activities during this period, as the civil rights movement peaked from 1955-1965. During this time, Congress passed the Civil Rights Act of 1964 and the Voting Rights Act of 1965, guaranteeing basic civil rights for all Americans, regardless of race. This victory only came after nearly a decade of nonviolent protests and marches, ranging from the 1955-1956 Montgomery bus boycott to the student-led sit-ins of the 1960s to the huge march on Washington in 1963.

Post-Civil Rights Generation

After the civil rights generation, the post-civil rights generation emerged. The post-civil rights generation represented people born between 1946 and 1964. They continued to advance civil rights and gain places of influence for African-Americans in government, corporate America and other sectors of society. This group also had to deal with fundamental issues facing minorities, such as economic hardship and inequality. Large sectors of these minority communities became economically irrelevant as more and more jobs began to require formal education and technical skills.

This was also the generation that began to reap the benefits of affirmative action and other rights for which the civil rights generation fought. Unfortunately, the authority of the church, according to some social analysts, weakened during this generation, especially among the urban poor. Statistically, Black church membership remained high during this time, but the nation began to see the moral climate change during this generation.

Hip-Hop Generation

The hip-hop generation is the current generation. They were born between 1965 and 1984. This is the generation that built the multi-billionaire-dollar-per-year hip-hop industry. By the 1990s, the African-American community had more financial opportunities than ever. Meanwhile, this generation became the "me" generation; it was no longer about building the Black community, but rather about doing for "me and mine."

With the absence of godly values and leadership amongst the members of this group, America quickly found itself experiencing a crisis, as high rates of homicide, suicide, imprisonment, single-parent homes, sexually transmitted diseases and other problems began to spread out of control. Meanwhile, hip-hop culture emerged as the dominant culture among this generation. Helped by the mass media, it is hard to go anywhere and not see the influence of hip-hop on this nation. Because hip-hop is both a musical style and a culture, it has established several corrupt cultural norms that contributed to changing the moral climate in this nation.

Generation Next

Last but not least, we have Generation Next, born between 1985 and the present. This will be the generation that comes after the hip-hop generation. Unfortunately, this future generation will be the product of the hip-hop generation's direct influence. This group of young people (ages 0 – 20 right now) will soon take over, without any clear expectations or direction. Worse yet, they will have little or no desire to serve God. If trends continue, America can expect only about 20 percent of the next generation to attend church. This nation can only wait and see what Generation Next will accomplish in the decades to come.

Seven Historical Reasons

Now that we have reviewed the five different 20th century generations, I will point out seven problems I've uncovered while studying these groups. The enumerated problems will partially explain why hip-hoppers do not attend church in higher numbers. I will identify not only problems, but also practical solutions to each of these problems, solutions that the church can use to attract more members of the current generation to Jesus Christ.

Problem #1: Because of the changing times, it is more difficult than ever for not only young adults to live for God, but for all people in general.

The post-slavery and the civil rights generations made sacrifices to make our world a better place. They were also a very religious people who wanted God in the center of their lives and struggles. The church was the foundation of the Black community back then. Consequently, people had real godly character during that time. I remember viewing videos of horrible images of African-Americans in the streets being attacked by police dogs, beaten upside the head by nightsticks, and being blasted with water hoses. The civil rights generation withstood these and other injustices so future generations could have opportunities they did not.

During the 70s, we witnessed a steady decline in moral values after the civil rights movement and during the post-civil rights generation, as people's mindsets shifted from doing what is best for "us" to doing what is best for "me." The hip-hop generation embraced similar values. The rights that were fought for by previous generations began to be treated with indifference by the hip-hoppers. Very few today understand the struggle it took to gain the rights that so many now freely enjoy. We once witnessed a group of people willing to fight for equality. Now we see a world where African-Americans kill each other over foolishness.

It is also clear that, as history progressed, God was gradually pushed further and further out of our society. The more our world has pushed God out, the more problems this nation has experienced. Looking at the present generations, who would ever have thought we would see rappers degrade women as they do, live in a world where it is common for 13-year-olds to be sexually active, or be faced with the lack of morality that can be witnessed every day on the evening news? Just when we think mankind has hit an all-time low, people seem to become even more immoral.

Remember when the high courts took prayer out of schools? Could we be headed toward a world that will ban Bible reading and take away other religious freedoms? Early in 2005, we saw the Supreme Court rule five to four that the framed Ten Commandments displayed in two Kentucky state courthouses violated the doctrine of separation of church and state. Also in September 2005, a federal judge ruled that the Pledge of Allegiance reference to one nation "under God" violates school children's right to be free from a coercive requirement to affirm God. Who knows, one of these days mankind might get so wicked that the courts will try to ban God totally.

Consequently, the time period we live in has effected how young people respond to God. The hip-hop generation lives in a world that does not respect God, so why should they respect Him? As our world becomes increasingly corrupt, we are going to see fewer people serving God. If we think the hip-hop generation is ungodly, we have not seen anything yet. Wait until Generation Next emerges.

Solution: It is important to have pastors and church leaders who understand the times in which we live. It is critical that they study not only the Bible, but also what is currently going on in our world. The world we live in is constantly changing. For example, there is no excuse for a pastor not to understand what hip-hop is and how it has impacted youth. Addressing many of the struggles of youth requires a level of understanding about their world. For example, it is foolish to think a parent can talk to their children about sex the same way their parents taught them. With so many new kinds of sexually transmitted diseases, misconceptions about sex (i.e., "A person cannot get an STD by having oral sex"), and issues like homosexuality, it is extremely important to stay informed and in touch with what is happening in our world today.

Problem #2: The church has produced very few leaders that the hip-hop generation esteem.

During the post-slavery and civil rights generations, most of the leaders within the Black community came from the church. Church was, by default, the social institution through which African-Americans could pursue social influence, power and leadership before the 1970s. This all shifted after the civil rights movement; because African-Americans suddenly had access to many different social and professional opportunities. Ultimately, this eroded the influence of the church within the Black community.

After the civil rights movement, the balance of power in the African-American community began to shift away from the church to other sectors of society. For instance, in 1965, there were about 100 elected Black officials in the United States. Presently, Black elected officials number about 9,000. This includes elected officials at all levels — federal, state and local. No longer is the clergy the leadership of choice for African-Americans. No longer can the church necessarily claim to be the primary leader within the African-

American community. Our nation has seen African-Americans rise to positions of influence in almost every sector of society.

It is hard to determine what came first. Did ungodly leadership in the Black community step up and lead, or did people choose ungodly leaders because they became more ungodly themselves? No matter how we look at this dilemma, it becomes clear that people during the 1970s did not want men of God leading them anymore. One of the reasons is that the moral climate shifted. We not only saw this in leadership, but in music, sexual behavior and other aspects of life. As godly men and women like Dr. Martin Luther King, Jr., Ralph David Abernathy, Fannie Lou Hamer and others from the church faded away in the 1970s, very few new leaders from the church stepped up to take their place.

Thus, when the Black community stopped looking toward the church for leadership, people like Minister Louis Farrakhan and Al Sharpton stepped up and helped to steer the Black community away from the church and Christian values. Today, the influence of Black clergy continues to fade among the hip-hop generation. Most hip-hoppers esteem people with no godly values. Ultimately, we become like those we follow or idolize. The hip-hop generation's leaders do not go to church, and so young people wonder why they should go themselves. Hip-hop stars like Jay Z, P. Diddy and Snoop Dogg are just some of the people with little or no moral integrity to whom young adults look up to. It is no wonder that so many young people are being led astray.

Solution: There is a great need for more Christian leaders with whom young people can identify and relate. If we examine the structure of most churches, a majority of their leaders are more than 40 years old. Unfortunately, many young people cannot and will not identify with many of these leaders. Members of the hip-hop generation want to see people who look like them and who have been through similar experiences.

The church's best bet is to send those in the church who came out of the hip-hop culture back into the community to reach those who need Christ. Hip-hoppers can relate to a Christian emcee more easily than they can to a typical pastor. The more churches are able to relate to these young people, the better the chance of reaching them. There are already some good urban ministries designed to reach the hip-hop generation. Christians should support and model those who are doing a good job of reaching this generation.

Problem #3: Fewer parents are raising godly children.

Family is one of the most essential elements in building a godly society. More young people than ever before are growing up in "broken" homes, and many parents are leaving the responsibility of raising godly children to the church, or simply making no effort at all to raise godly children. According to the Barna Research Group, having a significant faith commitment and an identifiable set of religious beliefs was mentioned by just one out of every five parents as an ingredient required for parental success. Only 22 percent of parents thought that it should be their first priority as a parent to enable their child to have a meaningful relationship with Jesus Christ.

Many of these parents do not have a strong relationship with God themselves, so they do not stress the importance of having one to their children. Apparently, the importance of being godly was not properly passed down from generation to generation. There was a time when mothers and grandmothers hauled their kids to church. These parents also prayed for their children and taught them godly values. They understood that it was their responsibility to raise godly children. The Bible says, "Train up a child in the way he should go: and when he is old, he will not depart from it" (Proverbs 22:6).

If a child witnesses little or no effort by their parents to live for God, they will most likely follow that same pattern. In other words, when a child sees a parent sleeping around, smoking weed, or cursing, they may well grow up embracing those non-Christian values. Many young people are growing up today thinking that church is only somewhere people go to on Sundays, and that

Christianity is not something we live out in our daily lives. These same young people grow up being the churchgoer who pops in and out of church a couple times of year or simply avoids church altogether.

The number of homes with two parents who both love God is small these days. Very few young people know what it means to have a godly father teaching them godly values or a mother they can observe being a godly woman. Consequently, many homes are producing young people who are growing up with little Biblical truth inside of them. It is no accident, then, that the music coming from the hip-hop community is immoral. The terrifying thing about this whole situation is that we are already experiencing the results of a generation that was not properly trained in the ways of God. Now these same individuals are parents themselves, raising the next generation. Ultimately, we are about to see even fewer young people growing up with any kind of Christian values.

Solution: The church should make it clear to parents that it is their responsibility to raise godly children, and should give them the tools to do so. How many churches have a ministry for parents? Should this not be a high priority in the church today? There is an immense need for mentorship programs for young men and women who do not have godly parents in the home. In some cases, the church has to act as a spiritual stepparent to many of these young people. This means working with youth all week long, and becoming involved with their lives outside of church.

Problem #4: The negative influences young people witness in the media have helped pull many young people away from God.

Over the years, the media has become a larger influence in each successive generation. For instance, the post-slavery generation did not have computers, television and all the technology that this generation has today. As time progressed, so did technology. We live in a time where a person can watch music videos on his or her cell phone or view pornography over the Internet. One of the reasons why hip-hop has been the most influential music ever is because we see it everywhere you go. It is almost impossible to screen people from this immoral culture. Consequently, there has never been a generation before this one that has been confronted by so many immoral images.

I remember reading an article in a hip-hop magazine offering advice to women on how to keep a man. The writer advised women that the best way to hold onto a man was to learn how to perform oral sex better. This is just one lie that young people hear and believe, a lie that is fed to them by the media every day. Unfortunately, no one is there to tell them the truth. Many parents are no longer the primary influences on their child, as many work and have other activities outside of the home. The negative rap music message often goes unchecked because young parents themselves are listening to it and don't see anything wrong with it. Meanwhile, young people are constantly receiving the message that living in sin is acceptable.

Most young adults are in the dark about just how much they are being influenced by the media. The reality is, whatever a person meditates on or looks upon is what he or she will soon become. Most young people are drawing role models from the people they see on television and listen to on the radio. They end up wanting to talk, dress, and act like the celebrities they see in the media. For instance, this generation sees rappers featured in videos with a drink in their hand surrounded by half-dressed women, and they end up wanting that out of life. Of course, they see very few people in the media who are living for Christ.

As young people witness fewer godly images in the media, Christianity becomes less appealing to them. This generation would rather take what the world has to offer them, instead of what God has to offer them. The media makes sin look so attractive that most watchers ignore its consequences and focus on its temporary rewards. They won't understand that living in sin will ultimately lead to death until they experience that reality for themselves.

Solution: Parents play a critical role in determining what does or does not influence their teens. Many parents are not helping their children make wise choices about the things they are allowing to influence them. Helping young people make choices is critical. The reality is that no matter how much we try to shield a young person from this ungodly culture, he or she will still be exposed to it. It would be great to see more films like *The Passion of the Christ* and other Christian alternatives that give young people choices in what they watch and listen to. With limited perceived options and not understanding the consequences of their decisions, young people will continue to be influenced by the media and to make bad choices.

Problem #5: These days, there are other activities besides church in which people can participate.

Life was once simpler than it is today. I remember hearing stories from my parents that there was actually a time when there were no video games and when very few homes in America had a television. Families actually spent quality time together. Developing a sense a family and community was a focal point in many communities. At the turn of the 20th century, all people really had was their family and their faith in God. Leisure time was often spent either with families or in church. Now, people are faced with many choices beyond church and family. There is more competition than ever for people's time and devotion.

In the 1960s, the church was the primary social intuition, outside of the family. It was not unusual for a church to offer at least three different services a week, and a weeklong revival once a month. It was also common for people to spend three or four hours in church on a Sunday morning, and to come back later that night for another three-hour service. Now, the average Christian does not want to spend more than three hours in church a week. There is a different mindset today than there was a couple of generations ago. There are more people who are working harder than ever to accomplish various goals, and they do not always take time to develop a relationship with God.

People are more success-driven today than in previous generations. In the past, people were more principle-driven. Thus, it was not difficult for them to follow the principles in the Bible. Today, people are more interested in building a successful career or business. Often, family and church are neglected. Fewer people understand how valuable it is to take the time to build a relationship with God. Spending all day in church has become a thing of the past. People now have places to go, people to see and things to do. In fact, some people would rather watch a sermon on television than drive to a church and sit through a service in person.

Church leaders have to be concerned that church will someday become obsolete, as our world becomes increasingly fast paced. People are being sucked into the rat race of life. The biggest problem is that people value material things more than they do God. Unfortunately, some people will continue to feel that they need to work harder, in order to afford a bigger house and a luxury car. As the price of gas, homes and other basic items continues to rise, so will people's need to work hard. Meanwhile, God and family will be neglected.

Solution: There is no easy solution to this problem. Let's face it, people now want what is convenient when it comes to Christianity. Some churches might want to consider offering an "express" service, as well as a traditional service. For that express service, the church should stress that people need not dress up. Part of the hassle of coming to church is getting ready. This service should be no longer than 90 minutes and very fast-paced and high-energy. Churches should also sell audio and videotapes as a way to get people to experience the word of God on a weekly basis. As they hear the Word prayerfully, many of these individuals will learn to make more time for God in their lives.

Problem #6: The hip-hop generation never embraced a corporate vision or faced challenges to overcome.

The hip-hop generation was one of the first generations without a corporate vision to act as a guiding force for a particular group to follow and focus on. For example, the post-slavery generation spent their time assisting African-Americans to successfully transition from slavery; the civil rights generation helped them gain civil rights; and the post-slavery generation helped them gain places of influence. As they struggled to accomplish their goals, there was a sense within each of these generations that they needed God in order to succeed.

For the most part, African-Americans were oppressed all the way through the post-slavery generation in the 1970s. The hip-hop generation did not have to deal with slavery, institutionalized racism or other major problems over which previous generations spent years on their knees before God praying about. Hip-hoppers have not encountered any obstacles so far-reaching that they have had to trust God to change. This is the generation that possesses the opportunities for which other generations spent decades fighting, and they have a chance to obtain quality educations, wealth and positions of influence. Unfortunately, instead of crying out to God in thanksgiving, they have rebelled against Him.

It is clear that oppression and uncertain times bring about a stronger intimacy with God. Remember when the planes crashed into the Twin Towers on September 11, 2001? Suddenly, many people started going to church. Then, when the threat was over, those same people stopped attending. This is exactly where the hip-hop generation is. I believe that slavery and oppression are two reasons why African-Americans traditionally have been the most religious people in this country.

Is not the hip-hop generation reminiscent of the children of Israel in the Bible? In the book of Exodus, the children of Israel cried out to God when they were in captivity. After God gave them their freedom, many of them strayed from God and began to worship other gods. The hip-hop generation has not handled freedom well. Much of the music we hear today from hip-hoppers comes out of ignorance and boredom. Without a clear vision of how to make a positive difference in the world, this generation appears to want to push God out of their lives. Of course, they will only do this until they need Him again. There are many in this generation who call on God, but they wait until they get into trouble to do so.

Solution: It is important that young people understand that God has a plan for their lives. Many young people are giving in to ungodly activities because they do not have a sense of direction and they are bored with life. Given the combination of boredom and little self-fulfillment, it is easy for many young people to get sucked into an immoral lifestyle. The statement, "if you do not stand for something, you will fall for anything," rings true here. Without a sense of direction, this generation is "falling for almost anything" like no generation before them.

Problem #7: The church stopped being aggressive and finding ways to relate to this generation.

Churches that go out to evangelize in their community with relevant ministry have pretty much gone out of style like polyester suits. There was a time when churches would hold revivals, and go out and persuade those in the community to come to the house of God. Not only that, many of these churches had quality relationships with non-parishioners in the community. Now, there are many pastors who seem to be content to take care only of their own members. Many churches have abandoned urban communities for the suburbs, leaving behind crime and liquor stores, and leaving very few people there to win back that community for Christ.

In the 1970s, when the churches started to move out of the Black community, the ungodly moved in. The time when people did not have to lock their doors came to an end as the churches' influence within the community started to decline. For many in the church today, the inner city is just a place we drive past on our way to work or church. The inner city is no longer a location where we go to share the gospel of Jesus Christ. Do not get me wrong; there are still many churches in some of these urban communities. However, most are not impacting their communities for Christ as they did before the 1970s.

As the Christian church became less aggressive, other religions became more aggressive recruiting in many of these communities.

For example, in the 1970s, the Nation of Islam went into the Black community and recruited thousands of men. At the same time, fewer men could be found in the Christian churches. The Nation of Islam developed an aggressive approach to recruiting men as they tapped into many of the needs of men within the Black community. Being aggressive in sharing the gospel will be one of the keys to getting many members of this present generation off the streets and into church. The hip-hop generation has been waiting for the church to come to them, while the church has been sitting back, waiting for the hip-hop generation.

The great commission is still going forward today, but in different ways. Many churches are taking advantage of Christian television networks, like TBN, as well as other media platforms. In my view, the church is trying to reach the world, but they are forgetting about the people. There was once a more grassroots effort to spread the gospel. Now, methods used by the church are so impersonal that the gospel is often ignored by most in this generation. There are fewer people engaging in face-to-face evangelism or developing ministries geared toward reaching the inner city. It is clear that many people are uneasy about confronting people concerning moral issues and reaching out to young adults. Yet, in a time when so many young people are looking for answers, the church continues to sit in the background regarding any action.

Solution: It is critical that the church be assertive and go into many of these communities to share the gospel. If people like Farrakhan can go out and recruit men into a religious organization, why cannot the church do the same? If Farrakhan can get one million men on the mall in Washington, D. C., there is no telling what Christians can do if they begin to combine their efforts in reaching more of this present generation. The church can, but as a whole has not. How many churches have a set strategy for how they plan to attract more of the hip-hop generation to church? The church won't accidentally reach people; it must assert itself to reach them.

Chapter 2

Ten Myths about Christianity

"I would rather live my life as if there is a God and die to find out there isn't, than live my life as if there isn't and die to find out there is."
- Albert Camus

Ten Misconceptions about Christianity

Many young adults have misconceptions about church that keep them away from the house of God. If the church hopes to attract hip-hoppers, they must deal with the different misconceptions that exist among the members of this generation. I will discuss what I believe are the 10 most popular misconceptions that prevent the hip-hop generation from serving God.

Misconception #1: Pastors build churches to gain wealth.

There are many in the hip-hop community who do not envision themselves donating to a church. Many hip-hoppers think that their money would be funding the expensive suits the pastor wears or the luxury car he drives. Members of the clergy who have been consumed by greed perpetrate young people's negative perceptions of pastors. There are too many pastors who live self-indulgent lifestyles today. In addition, far too many church leaders have been caught stealing from their own churches. It only takes a couple of dishonest pastors to give church leaders across the country an awful name.

The reality is that church is one of the easiest places for corruption to exist. Why? Many churches have little or no accountability when it comes to money. Taking all this into consideration, it is imperative that church leaders be modest in the way they dress and in the cars they drive. Hip-hoppers might not understand why they see a pastor constantly wearing a $2,000 suit or driving a $50,000 car. Even as more pastors are becoming wealthy from preaching the gospel, it is important that they be sensible in this area.

Too many members of the hip-hop generation already think that life is about obtaining money and material things. However, many of those young people end up looking good on the outside and feeling empty on the inside. They do not see that buying a car they cannot afford is not the answer to insecurity. So what kind of message is it sending when nonbelievers witness parishioners consumed by having nice clothing, new cars and other material things, instead of being content with having a relationship with Jesus Christ?

There is also a concern about how some pastors raise the offering during a Sunday service. Most nonbelievers think that Christians are being manipulated into giving the pastor as much money as they can. Some of the techniques pastors use to obtain money from their congregation seem a little unethical, even to the most mature believer. What will a young person think when they see the unsavory methods some pastors use to fill the collection plates?

I do believe that people should be taught the value of giving. Yet, too many churches play on people's emotions to solicit donations. Because many young people think they are serving a man and not God, they will not put more than a dollar in the church's collection plate. They do not understand that every time a person gives to a church, he or she is actually giving to God.

Solution: The church needs to cut off all the avenues where young people may suspect underhanded dealings. There needs to be a stronger level of accountability, when it comes to the church and money. In addition, it would help to have more open lines of communication between church leaders and the congregation. Many people come off the streets with trust issues, so it is important that the church be aware of these issues and plan for them. Until trust is developed, the church will continue to see young people spend most of their money on themselves and give very little to the church.

Misconception #2: The church doesn't care about the community.

Realistically speaking, most nonbelievers understand that some churches collect millions of dollars from their congregation each year. Many ask themselves, "How much of that money is going to actually contributing to evangelical pursuits?" For example, I wonder how much money the church gave to the victims of Hurricane Katrina in New Orleans in the summer of 2005. When nonbelievers detect few programs designed to reach and help people, they get suspicious. Many people are tired of the building funds and other programs designed to build bigger churches. Many hip-hoppers feel it is the church's job to help make a positive impact in the community.

There was a time when people would seek out churches to donate to because of the work they were doing in the community. Nowadays, people would much rather give their money to organizations like the Red Cross or the United Way. There was also a time when people in the community who were not members of the church would run to the church in a crisis. Today, it seems that some churches are too busy to give even their members help, let alone the community.

The way people look at church has changed over the years. Consequently, most communities do not want churches in their neighborhoods anymore. In some communities, churches are causing more problems then they have solved. On Sunday mornings, church members around the country can be found parking illegally, littering, and being rude. Over the years, there has been a growing number of communities protesting the presence of churches in their neighborhoods for these and other reasons.

Most communities would rather have a supermarket or a department store in their midst. At least these businesses bring jobs to the community. They ask themselves, "What does building another church bring to the community but more headaches?" This all stems from the growing perception most hip-hoppers have that the church is no longer helping people in need.

Solution: If people saw the church leaders and parishioners rolling up their sleeves and helping others, the church would re-establish creditability in most communities. Nonbelievers are not impressed with the church's large concerts and church services. They want to see the church providing some real solutions and reaching out to the needy in their community. It would be great to see people calling the local pastor for help, instead of calling their councilman. But first the church must show that it cares. If people do not feel like they can run to the church for help, they will not run to the church at all.

Misconception #3: The church is out of touch.

There are many young adults who choose to seek comfort in a bottle of liquor or in illegal drugs, rather than going to church for help. There is also a growing number of young people who would rather read a daily horoscope or get a palm reading than read the Bible. Their "churches" end up being nightclubs and local hangout spots where hip-hoppers come together and deal with their problems in an ungodly way. Young adults today are trying anything and everything to obtain direction in life or a sense of peace. Why? There are more people than ever who perceive the church as being out of touch with what is really going on in our world today.

Some nonbelievers think that church is a place to go to hear some good singing and inspirational preaching. At most, they expect to get a quick emotional high while in church, but little or nothing else. As a matter of fact, most people view what they see in church as almost comical. They feel that the church will not meet their needs. It can be frustrating to leave the church Sunday after Sunday with the same problems and without any real sense of hope in sight. This is a reality for many young people, and it drives them to seek answers in other places.

This is the generation that refuses to come to church out of tradition. They are seeking real answers from God. In past generations, people attended church because it was the "right" thing to do. This trend has been a good thing and a bad thing at the same time. It has been bad because many people have sat in church for years and have never had a true, life-changing experience with God. The issues they came into the church with are the same issues they have carried with them for years. Today, if the church does not give this generation real solutions and answers, they will leave and seek answers somewhere else!

Solution: On an average Sunday, do we witness young people crying out at the altar for God, homosexuals who want to repent, or neighborhood drug dealers who want to give their lives to church? If young people came to church and had a life-changing experience, they would be more motivated to return. Nowadays, people are tired of going through the motions and seemingly wasting a couple hours on a Sunday morning in church. The more practical solutions the church can provide, the better. But first, the church leaders should make sure they understand the needs of the hip-hop generation.

Misconception #4: There are too many gays in the church.

In many Black churches, in particular, we might see someone leading the choir who is a homosexual, or see some throughout the congregation. Coincidently, there is a growing perception in many young people's minds that the church has become a safe haven for gays. In some churches, we see very few masculine young men who are whole-heartedly serving God. Men from off the street see what kind of men are within the church, and do not think they fit into that environment. Many men who oppose the homosexual lifestyle do not always feel comfortable worshipping alongside someone who is gay.

Some pastors see the congregation filled with people struggling with homosexuality, but neglect to address it or do not know how.

Some church leaders even promote these individuals to leadership positions in the church. In my view, the church should welcome homosexuals with open arms. Regardless of the sin a person is struggling with, the church should be there to help. I also think that the leadership of a church should send a clear message to the congregation that God hates homosexuality but loves homosexuals.

Many young people think that the church is hypocritical in this area. If a pastor is preaching against homosexuality in the pulpit one Sunday, and then turns to a gay choir director to lead the choir in a song, what does that say to the rest of the congregation? I also think it is the church's responsibility to address myths about being gay, like "people are born that way."

The biggest problem I see is when pastors know someone is struggling with homosexuality issues and still promotes them to a position of influence in the church. For example, I have seen gay men preside over the men's ministry at particular churches. Is it a surprise that most men in that particular ministry will end up being gay? Often, the followers reflect their leaders. Groups like the Nation of Islam attract strong, masculine men, while it is becoming a trend for the Christian church to attract more feminine men. If a church wants to attract strong, masculine, godly men, those are the type of men the church needs to put into leadership positions.

Even though most churches' leadership is dominated by men, males who attend church regularly tend to fall under 14 years of age or over 60. Boys come because their mothers make them attend, and older men often establish church membership when their health begins to fail. Adult women, particularly those over 40, form the backbone of many churches. Pastors have to be concerned about the lack of men in the house of God. The church has to find a way to do a better job of attracting masculine men.

Solution: This is not an easy topic to discuss. There is a fine line between accepting gays in the church and simply accepting their behavior. Saying all of this, one thing the church cannot do is compromise the word of God. We live in a day when public schools are under increasing pressure to accept curriculum materials that promote homosexuality as a normal (even desirable) alternative lifestyle. It is important that the church stand firm on this issue, because the pressure to compromise will only get worse. If the church compromises, there is no question that the world will as well.

Misconception #5: God does not love me.

There are many young people who have come from abusive backgrounds, having been molested or abandoned as a child, and made to feel like a piece of junk. All their lives, they have been sent the message by different people they have encountered that they are worthless. They think to themselves, "How can God possibly love me and allow 'this' to happen to me?" We all have had a "this" in our lives that effected our self-esteem. Most young people have these types of questions, which often go unanswered. Some have never had a family to show them love and attention, or to help them find a sense of identity.

We often underestimate the power of love. When a person does not love who they are or does not think anyone else loves them, low self-esteem begins to dictate how they view life. Not only do they not love themselves, they also do not see how God can possibly love someone like them. It is surprising how many young people engage in risky behavior because they never discovered that God loves them. Many young people would rather slowly kill themselves using drugs, having unprotected sex, or running the streets looking for trouble, instead of dealing with who they really are.

As long as they think God does not care about their lives, some of them will never come to church. So many young people end up in clubs, in the arms of the opposite sex, or any place they can find love. This is the reason young boys join gangs or young girls sleep with anybody who shows them attention. Unfortunately, many of these young people are looking toward almost every source but the church, as they try to find love. Many in the hip-hop generation do not associate the church with love. That is why a person in this situation often gravitates to the first person or group who they feel can show them love. Often times, this ends up being an abusive relationship.

Solution: Going out and sharing the love of Jesus Christ with a young person is something that can be more valuable than preaching to them about their immoral lifestyle. Many in the hip-hop generation act the way they do because they do not love themselves. When young people do not know what love is, they will settle for almost anything that looks like love. The church needs to be the standard as far as love is concerned. Nonbelievers should be able to see the church giving without any thought of return.

Misconception #6: Most Christians are just as sinful as I am.

Back in the day, attending church meant something. Now, it means absolutely nothing in this generation's eyes. It is hard to distinguish between the hypocrites in the church and the Christians who are going through the process of becoming more like Christ. We also live in a time when it is difficult to distinguish between a mature Christian and the average person who does not have a relationship with Jesus Christ. Many believers focus on just attending church instead of allowing God to transform their lives. Consequently, the hip-hop generation often witnesses hypocrites within the house of God.

We live in a day where many people want to preach but very few want to live out the word of God. There are some nonbelievers who think most Christians are living double lifestyles. In other words, they think that, on Sunday, most believers are praising God in church but that during the week, they are living a lifestyle unbecoming of a Christian. Nonbelievers are not shocked anymore when they see Christians behaving as badly as they do. Many nonbelievers feel that at least they are being true to themselves by totally living out in the world instead of "faking it" in church.

With all the hypocrisy in the church, people do not have any respect for Christians, the church or what the church stands for anymore. Christians who live a compromised lifestyle perpetuate this idea. In addition, this generation has seen people like R. Kelly and Michelle Williams of Destiny's Child claim Christ as their savior but write songs that are leading people into sin. The more people this generation sees compromising, the less they take Christianity seriously. They figure if Christians do not take their relationship with God seriously, why should they take Christianity seriously?

Solution: When the hip-hop generation sees churches not committed to the principles of the Bible, they lose respect for the body of Christ. For instance, I have seen churches passing out condoms and talking to young people about having safe sex. These and other behaviors send a mixed message to young people about how serious the church is about following the word of God. Many churches are beginning to perform gay marriages and involving themselves in other ungodly things. People need to see a church that is standing firm on the word of God. Even if the world hates the church, if the church stands firm, they will at least respect it.

Misconception #7: Jesus is my friend and not my Lord.

Nowadays, it has become a trend for hip-hop and rhythm and blues artists to have a couple of tracks on their album about Jesus. Of course, the rest of the album is usually glorifying sin. This is a reflection of how this generation feels about God. It has become trendy to have a little religion in your life. Whether wearing a chain with a cross on it, thanking God at the Grammy Awards, or doing the "church thing" every once in a while, many young people are expressing religion. Most people want some kind of relationship with God. Why? They need someone to call on in times of trouble. They look at Jesus as their buddy who can get them out of a "jam" now and then.

Hip-hoppers generally do not understand that Jesus Christ is not their friend; He wants to be their Lord. Many in this generation have no problem with Jesus Christ until it is time for them to submit to Him. People like these, when asked about Christ, give a bunch of super-spiritual answers about God and the church. For example, they will state that a Christian really does not need to go to church to "be in good" with God. What they are really saying is that they want God without the commitment. So they do what they want to do. When it's time to deal with the consequences of their choices, all of a sudden they want to involve God. This is a constant pattern in many hip-hoppers' lives.

This generation does not fear God as past generations have. I often witness rap artists giving God the middle finger or disrespecting Him in their songs. At times, I ask myself whether these rappers really know what they are doing. The reality is, most members of this generation do not. They think God is some soft, old man dressed in all white with a long beard who will not someday judge them for their ungodly behavior. They know nothing about the God of the Old Testament who has promised judgment upon all those who rejected His son.

Solution: This generation not only needs to know that God loves them, but that they will have to give account for their lives one day. There are many churches that simply talk about the love and grace of God, and not about His wrath and jealousy. The reality is that God hates sin. A person would not know this from listening to the average pastor nowadays. Ultimately, God wants to be first in our lives. This is a reality that needs to be communicated to the present generation.

Misconceptions #8: Christianity is the white man's religion.

There are actually some within the hip-hop generation who are still angry about what white people did to African-Americans in the past. These are individuals who have a problem with the white-skinned and blue-eyed image of Jesus Christ, and the fact that white folks forced Christianity on African-Americans during slavery. Consequently, they think that Christianity is the white man's religion, and that African-Americans have no business participating in it. These are the type of people who have trouble letting go of the past, and end up aligning themselves with the Nation of Islam and other Black organizations. Some of these individuals see the white man as their adversary. Ultimately, before they are anything in life, they think they are Black.

Members of this generation buy into many of these different beliefs because they are angry inside and are looking for someone to blame for their problems. They do not understand that it is their decisions that will determine success or failure in life. Thus, some point the finger at white America and do not take responsibility for their lives. Many leaders in the Black community continue to throw salt on these wounds, with movements like the Reparation Movement. Meanwhile, the hip-hop generation continues to sink lower in irresponsibility, following this line of thinking communicated to them by many of these Black organizations. For example, someone needs to hold these men accountable for having all these babies out of wedlock.

People like Louis Farrakhan, leader of the Nation of Islam, have long expressed anti-Semitic and anti-white rhetoric. The Nation of Islam leader once said, "White people are potential humans…They have not evolved yet." These and other hate-filled comments have helped to define Farrakhan and his organization. So why have many Black pastors supported his different causes? Pastors often send mixed messages to the world when they link up with people like Farrakhan. In my view, Christians have no business supporting events like the Million Man March and other activities that do not fall in line with the word of God.

Solution: It is the church's job to stress love, forgiveness and hope for a brighter future, not to team up with groups like the Nation of Islam who practice hate and condemnation. How Christians deal with racial issues should be different from how Muslim organizations like the Nation of Islam do. When the church joins with people like Farrakhan, it is validating what he stands for. The world needs more people willing to love and not hate. Meanwhile, the church needs to break down many of the misconceptions that divide people. It is heartbreaking that there is still a lack of racial diversity in most churches.

Misconception #9: I need to get my life together before I come to God.

There is a term many in the hip-hop generation use, called "keeping it real." When a young person is keeping it real, his or her actions on the outside reflect how he or she feels on the inside. Most of us call "keeping it real" having a sense of integrity. This is one reason why some young people look up to stars like Allen Iverson and Snoop Dogg. They think these individuals are keeping it real by still wearing cornrows and promoting an ungodly lifestyle, even though they are celebrities. These individuals feel like they cannot simultaneously attend church and keep it real out in the streets.

Many of these young people feel a commitment to the streets. They feel that, if they turn their backs on the streets, they will be a "sell-out." Even thought they know that the street life is not ideal, it is as if they have taken an oath to stay there. Some would rather do that than live as a good Christian. They see Jesus Christ as a good thing, but not for them right now. Thus, there is an ongoing battle inside of them. They have questions like the following: What will my friends think? Will God accept me in my present state? What will the church think about my current lifestyle? They do not understand that a person comes to Christ first and then changes. They want to get their lives together first. In reality, they do not want to deal with the responsibilities of being a Christian.

There is no proper time for someone to give his or her life to Christ, other than the present. Many of us know that tomorrow is not promised to anyone. Yet, a lot of young people do not think about death and eternity, so they continue as though they have plenty of time to give their lives to Christ. The reality is that some make a commitment to Christ in time and others do not. Many in the hip-hop generation have a mentality that only allows them to see the here and now. They will worry about the future when it arrives.

Solution: Christianity is supposed to be a daily journey where God molds a person into the image of Christ through daily devotion to His word. For those who believe that it is their job to get their own life together, they need to know that it is God's power, not our own, that changes our lives. This type of individual has good intentions. However, they also need to know that good intentions will not get anyone into Heaven. They need to see that the commitments they have are not greater than the commitment they need to make.

Misconception #10: Christianity is a set of rules designed to strip me of all of my fun.

Many in the hip-hop generation want to wait until they are older before they make a commitment to God. Many in this category are hurting inside and do not see that their current sinful lifestyle is contributing to that pain. They continue to drink, smoke, and have sex, thinking that these actions will take away their suffering. These and other activities in which young people engage only offer a temporary solution. They do not understand that Jesus Christ is the answer. All they see are the rules they will have to follow if they decide to live for Christ. This kind of individual probably thinks that life is about having as much fun as they can before they die. They often deem Christians as being foolish for living righteously.

Many of these individuals have no fear of God or of going to Hell. As a matter of fact, some in this generation think that hell will be a place where they can smoke weed, have sex, and continue to party. In other words, they think that they will be able to spend eternity doing whatever they want to do. This often stems from the authority issues that some young people struggle with today, as many grew up in homes with no authority figure. They end up having no desire to attend church and deal with all its rules. Even if this type does attend church, they often times do not stay. These individuals do not want be confronted about issues in their life, put to work, or asked to submit to the leadership in the church.

We cannot totally blame them for not wanting to serve God. Part of this misconception comes from watching Christians who are not enjoying life themselves. Thus, a lot of young people tell themselves they do not want to end up living a life similar to the lives that those Christians are living. They would rather live like 50 Cent or Beyonce Knowles, acquiring power, money and respect. Deep inside, we all want to live life to its fullest. Most nonbelievers look at the average Christian and do not want what they have. It is almost as though they see Christianity as an ailment.

Solution: It is important that Christians not stress the "rules" of the Bible, but rather stress having a relationship with Christ. A commitment to follow rules will be a byproduct after a person develops a relationship with Jesus Christ. If they quit focusing on rules, some will see the benefits of following them and the consequences if they do not. Most young people do not see the consequences of their behavior clearly, or walk around with a this-can't-happen-to-me mentality. Only when they have to deal with their decisions in life do they begin to value rules.

Chapter 3

The Hip-Hop Generation

"Don't do drugs, don't have unprotected sex, and don't be violent. Leave that to me."

- Eminem

As we continue to examine why the hip-hop generation does not serve God, I think it will be helpful to examine hip-hop itself. In Chapters 1 and 2, we examined the changing seasons of the Black church from a historic perspective, as well as 10 misconceptions hip-hoppers have about church. Now that we have an idea how this generation came to be, we will look at some of today's trends that have influenced this generation, how the church has responded, and the potential solutions.

Brief History

Hip-hop began in New York in the 1970s. Jamaican-born DJ Kool Herc moved to New York in the late 1960s and brought with him the Jamaican tradition of "toasting," which involved reciting improvised rhymes over instrumental sections of reggae records. He used twin turntables and cut back and forth between two separate records to create a new sound. *Rapper's Delight* by the Sugar Hill Gang was one of the first rap recordings. It became a huge international hit and went on to become the best-selling 12-inch record ever, selling more than two million copies worldwide. This is where the term "hip-hop" was coined. Utilizing beats from a wide variety of sources, such as old gospel, jazz, James Brown/Motown soul, funk, disco and drum machines, and then remixing them, became known as sampling – the musical core of hip-hop.

Over the years, hip-hop grew into an international success, and it's still going strong today. It managed to survive the untimely deaths of rap stars such as Notorious B.I.G. and 2Pac, and shifted to a new focus. Although artists such as Jay-Z and Snoop Dogg gained commercial success while maintaining their street creditability, hip-hop became a marketing product. Rappers are becoming CEOs, starting clothing lines (Sean John), and owning film companies. With artists such as Nelly, Eminem, Lil Bow Wow and many others, hip-hop could be here for the long run.

Hip-hop has taken over the young people of America. Last year (2004), Edison Media Research conducted a national survey of 12 to 24 year olds. In that survey, the research company described 10 general kinds of music and asked the respondents how often they listened to each type. Hip-hop basically demolished any other musical category. Just under half of all the respondents said that they listen to hip-hop frequently (49 percent). The next closest music types were R&B and alternative rock, which tied at 34 percent. Hip-hop and rap proved equally popular for young men and young women, and was only slightly more popular with the 12- to 17-year-old range than with the 18 to 24 year olds. While it is much more popular with African-Americans and Hispanics, hip-hop and rap are still by far the most popular musical type among whites between 12 and 24 as well.

One reason why this type of music is so popular today is because it offers urban youths a chance to freely express how they feel. There are very few rules in hip-hop; just be original. A person can rap about anything – a car, feelings, relationships – anything. Unfortunately, although hip-hop originated in the inner city's negative cash-flow system of hustling, pushing, pimping, and banging, it became a multi-billion-dollar business. As hip-hop has become integrated into the popular culture medium, many knew that it had the potential either to help, through education and setting positive norms and actions, or to hinder its listeners from progressing and obtaining any moral character.

The Impact of Hip-Hop

More than any music in the past, hip-hop expresses mainstream American ideas that have now been internalized and embedded into the psyches of many young adults and youths. We have seen styles of music come and go, but there has never been a music that made such an impact as hip-hop has. Unfortunately, this impact has been a negative one. Let's look at some of the detrimental trends hip-hop has perpetuated over the years.

Because hip-hop is both music and culture, it has established several corrupt cultural norms. For instance, all women, but particularly Black women, are seen in popular hip-hop culture as sex objects. Almost every hip-hop video that is regularly aired today shows many dancing women (usually surrounding one or two men), wearing not much more than two-piece swimsuits, with the cameras focusing on their body parts. These images accompany explicit lyrics that commonly contain degrading comments suggesting that women are not worth anything more than money, if that.

Many Black men within the hip-hop culture have been conditioned by society not to trust or love. After all, if they do not love themselves, it is difficult for them to love women or anyone else in a healthy manner. Women use men to obtain money and material things, and men use women for sex. Therefore, once a man acquires all the sex he wants from a woman, he leaves, only to try to sleep with another woman.

Women do the same when it comes to money. The more money a man has, the more he is sought after within the Black community. His wealth overpowers other potential qualities of his moral character; the way he treats women or the fact he may be a career criminal are ignored when it comes to picking a mate. Marriage is something not highly valued in this group.

It is common for a man in the hip-hop culture to sleep with more than 20 or 30 women in a year. For many men, this is how they build their self-esteem. The more women a man can sleep with, the better he feels about himself, and the more he is respected among his peers. Unfortunately, this negative trend has caused many women to raise multiple babies without a man in the home, and sexually transmitted disease to run rampant in communities. This cycle is encouraged by the music that most hip-hoppers listen to, as many of the songs contain explicit lyrics about sex. Here is an example of lyrics a person will commonly hear in a hip-hop song:

> *In the club on the late night, feelin' right/ Lookin', tryin' to spot somethin' real nice/ Lookin' for a little shorty, hot and horny, so that I can take home/ She can be 18 wit' an attitude or 19, kinda snotty, actin' real rude/ Boo, as long as you a thicky, thicky, thick girl, you know that it's on.* – Nelly

Another trend I have noticed in studying the hip-hop culture is that its members tend to value short-term gratification over long-term success. Many in the hip-hop generation will sink all their money into things like clothing, jewelry and nice cars. Obtaining material wealth seems to be a priority even if illegal activity is involved. For many young people, money makes the world go around. Obtaining a quality education and being altruistic and hard working are often frowned upon by many the in hip-hop culture. Consequently, there are many young people who face ridicule if they excel in school. Even sadder, in some communities it is common for a person to be given respect if he has been in prison. This is what some call having street credibility.

In general, hip-hop artists have no respect for God and His principles. We can often witness hip-hop artists like Jay Z, Eminem and other rappers disrespecting God in their songs and videos. Indirectly, they are encouraging their listeners to do the same. Hip-hop also teaches its supporters to be prideful. This can be seen as some artists give their listeners the appearance that they are gods, mocking the true and living God. What many of these rappers are looking for is worship from their fans. Here is an example of some disrespectful lyrics. Keep in mind that Ja Rule is talking about himself:

> *For he so feared the word/ He left his only begotten son/ To shed his blood/ Show that pain is love/ But I won't cry/ Cause I live to die/ Wit my mind on my money/ And my guns in the sky.* – Ja Rule

In previous generations, serving God was part of the culture. For instance, at the turn of the 20th century, during the post-slavery generation, we saw in Chapter 1 how God was a vital part of people's lives. Christianity helped many African-Americans heal from the pain of slavery and move forward into freedom. In their generation, a person was looked down on if he or she did not have a relationship with God. Now, almost a century later, we have arrived at a place where young people face a culture that looks down on them if they do serve God. This is one reason why America can expect only about 20 percent of the next generation to attend church.

The Church and Hip-Hop

The church has been silent over the years, with respect to hip-hop. Yet, there have been some who have spoken out. Rev. Calvin Butts, pastor of Harlem's Abyssinian Baptist Church, declared in a 2000 PBS documentary that hip-hop was "the Devil's music." He went on say, "Unless we speak against this [rap music], it will creep continually into our society and destroy the morals of our young people." Even though I do not totally agree with his statements, I believe that Rev. Butts has been one of the few in the body of Christ who has taken a public stance against hip-hop. In many respects, Rev. Butts represents how the typical pastor has responded to the hip-hop generation.

Some church leaders see the problem but do not understand enough to really provide quality solutions. The result is that they are being written off as being "out of touch." For example, let's examine Rev. Butts' statements. Is hip-hop truly the Devil's music, or is it a music that the Devil has used to pull young people away from Christ? See, there is a considerable difference between something belonging to the Devil and being a tool the Devil simply uses. The Bible does declare that the Devil is a thief. No matter what we believe about hip-hop, it is vital that the church communicate the right messages and brainstorm quality strategies to end this dilemma.

Church leaders can burn all the hip-hop CDs they want, but young people will continue to buy the music if there is no change inside of them. Simply speaking out against hip-hop has not worked. The record sales tell us this. In 2004, according to SoundScan, R&B singer Usher sold nearly eight million copies of his album, "Confessions." This was the top-selling album in 2004. Also in 2004, sales of hip-hop CDs alone topped $1.5 billion and annual sales of hip-hop clothing was $2.5 billion. Related hip-hop merchandising and marketing reached $1.7 billion. Moreover, 42 percent of songs in the weekly Billboard Top 20 charts that mention brand names were hip-hop. In 2005, 50 Cent's "The Massacre" sold almost six million copies in just six months.

Solution

This book is really about culture and its impact on people's lives. We have the problems we find today because over the years we saw a major shift in the moral climate as the culture changed. Now we are moving closer to a world that no longer wants God as part of it, and so it is important for the church to focus on influencing our culture. Simply getting rid of hip-hop is not the answer. Even if hip-hop died today, young people would just find other ways to express themselves in an ungodly way. Hip-hop is just a symptom of a larger problem. This is why I have adopted an if-you-can't-beat-them-you-might-as-well-join-them mentality. In other words, Christians need to infuse hip-hop with God's holiness through their words and actions. The church will probably never take down hip-hop, so it is wise to finds ways to influence the culture instead.

Keep in mind that there is nothing wrong with hip-hop itself. The problem is how people use it. Over the years, hip-hop has been utilized for various purposes. When hip-hop first began in the 1970s, it gave young people a way to express the conditions of the urban community. In the 1980s, artists like Public Enemy and KRS ONE used this particular platform to educate listeners about real issues like racism and police brutality. Unfortunately, during the 1990s, rappers such as NWA and Ice T used hip-hop to glorify sex, drugs and violence. Notice, as the times changed, so did the music. Today many hip-hop artists continue to misuse the music as they promote promiscuity and material wealth. Why can't Christians use hip-hop to put God back into our culture?

For years, people have tried to speak out against hip-hop, without getting to the root of this dilemma. This is one reason why I have spent more than five years editing a Christian hip-hop magazine. I believe a person can only fight culture with culture. What I and others have done is use hip-hop to present Christian values to young people. If the church hopes to change culture, they need to use tools like hip-hop music to saturate this generation with the word of God. This fight can be won, but one thing the church cannot afford to do is sit back and wait on something supernatural to happen. As we studied history earlier in this book, we learned that things are getting progressively worse, while Christians have become progressively more passive.

Chapter 4

Reaching the Hip-Hop Culture

"I'd rather have people hate me with the knowledge that I tried to save them."

– Keith Green

Reaching the Hip-Hop Culture

In the first three chapters of this book, I examined reasons why the hip-hop generation does not serve God. In this chapter, we are going to focus on particular solutions and ministries who are actually reaching the hip-hop generation. The fact that hip-hop as a culture deals with the lives of underclass groups should lead us to examine approaches Jesus used in dealing with the poor, the hurting and the outcasts of His day. As one searches the scriptures, it is clear that Jesus did use different approaches to reach different people. It is also clear that He met people where they were, even though many people He encountered had different cultural backgrounds than He did. For example, Jesus ministered to a Samaritan woman, even though He was Jewish (John 4:4-26).

When one sees hip-hop as a culture, new doors are opened to reach those who are influenced by it. Hip-hop allows Christians in contemporary culture to be as the Apostle Paul was when he addressed the altars built to unknown gods and used them as vehicles to present the true God who can be known intimately through Jesus Christ (Acts 17:22-24). Keep in mind, God can use anything to present the truth of the gospel message. Hip-hop is just one of His latest tools.

There are actually numerous churches and Christian organizations that are currently doing a good job reaching the hip-hop generation. We will first look at some of these ministries and the methods they currently employ which have allowed them to successfully reach urban youths. While you read, hopefully some of these ministries will stimulate ideas and furnish a better understanding of what it takes to reach urban youths.

Examples of Effective Ministries

Crossover Church (www.flavoralliance.com)

The Crossover Church in Tampa, Florida, pastored by Urban D., has done an excellent job at reaching the hip-hop generation. They use hip-hop culture through fashion to create a "dressed-down" environment where people do not feel less important in church if they do not come wearing a suit and tie. In this way, hip-hop culture becomes a vehicle for communicating the gospel and relating to youths who have come out of that particular culture. They also use spoken word, dance, rap, skateboarding and the visual arts to present Biblical truths. More than 200 young people come each week to worship God, with a deejay and Christian emcees leading worship. Hip-hop is being employed to create a new culture for the emerging Christ-centered, multiethnic and urban community.

Street Life (www.thealabamabaptist.org)

Street Life, a Christian outreach program for young people in Houston's urban hip-hop culture, offers a distinctive blend of student ministry, evangelism, church planting and discipleship. The hip-hop approach operates on two fronts. Hard-edged, streetwise entertainment with a distinctively redemptive message draws non-Christian young people. Then small groups offer them a place to experience community, encounter the gospel message, and develop into disciples. Street Life churches also use rap music, soulful rhythm and blues, stand-up comedy and dramatic films to package the gospel in such a way that an urban generation raised on the streets will receive the word of God.

In part, this is accomplished through relationships built in small groups, where non-Christians can talk frankly to mature

Christians about issues that matter to them. But first, Christians have to establish a rapport with them by approaching them on common ground. Just as Jesus ministered among prostitutes, tax-gatherers, lepers and other outcasts, Street Life is meeting people where they are – in the hip-hop culture. This particular ministry has impacted thousands of lives using these techniques.

Club 3 Degrees (www.club3degrees.com)

There are also Christian nightclubs around the country that are doing a good job reaching urban youths. At Christian nightclubs like Club 3 Degrees – believed to be the largest and longest-running of the bunch – churchgoers can gather and groove in an environment free of the perceived sinfulness of secular spots. Though there is no industry group to track the growth of such clubs, anecdotal evidence suggests that they are proliferating in cities like Dallas, Nashville and, most recently, Tampa. They range from small coffeehouses to cavernous concert halls.

These outreaches have all the elements of traditional clubs, but without the alcohol, dirty dancing and violence. Usually, there is a deejay that plays urban gospel tunes most of the night, as young people praise and worship God in the form of dance. In addition, these clubs feature Christian performers. It is an opportunity for young people to have fun and be in an atmosphere where the gospel is being shared. Another benefit of clubs like Club 3 Degrees is that it gives nonbelievers an opportunity to experience the gospel of Jesus Christ in a nontraditional church environment. This is an important facet, as many in the hip-hop generation do not want to attend a traditional church.

Urban Change (www.urbanchange.net)

Urban Change uses the arts, support groups and workshops to reach youth. Through seminars, stage plays, retreats, videos and books, Urban Change is committed to bringing wisdom and knowledge to communicate God's word all across the United States. I had the opportunity to attend one of their stage plays,

Sexpose. This play included a talented array of actors, singers, poets and musicians. The compelling plotline resembled a daytime soap, but the goal was to reveal the behaviors and circumstances that lead to extra-marital sex and its life-altering consequences. At the performance I attended, more than 100 young people gave their lives to Christ. This is an achievement we rarely see in traditional church environments.

The American Bible Society (www.americanbible.org)

The American Bible Society (ABS) has developed a unique youth ministry program entitled Elementz of Life (EOL). It uses media such as art, music, dance and edgy youth resources to present the scriptures in compelling and contemporary ways. EOL allows ABS to expand its reach to a new audience and make a greater impact on communities and young people. The literature they release gives young people a contemporary look at the scriptures and puts the Bible in a language they can understand.

The Impact Movement (www.impactmovement.com)

The Impact Movement is a movement of young Christians (18-25 years old) committed to making an impact on their community and the world. They engage youth, college students and emerging professionals with the gospel. They exist to serve and to work in cooperation with, and in support of, the African-American church with programs that include a fellows program for college ministries and national networks of those engaged in youth and young adult ministry. This organization also hosts conferences to energize young people to go out and evangelize in their community, and they have about 20 chapters of campus ministries around the country.

Amen Films (www.holyhiphop.com/holyhiphopmovie.htm)

There are a growing number of films designed to reach urban youths with the gospel of Jesus Christ. Christopher Martin, executive director of Amen Films and founder and CEO of HP4 Digital Works and Solutions, is producing a film about Christian hip-hop. Since Mel Gibson's *Passion of the Christ*, the global audience has exploded for Christian inspirational films and music worldwide. This movie delves into aspects of the rapidly rising Christian hip-hop music genre and the global movement focused on street ministry evangelism.

Mercy Street Ministry (www.mercystreet.com)

This ministry is committed to sharing the message of Christ with all people. Through actual street witnessing, training of churches and Web-based training, they hope that someone who otherwise would never have known Christ will find Him as their Savior. People in 66 nations and 48 states in America have been trained by the Street University. Every day, there are witnesses all over the world using the simple techniques contained within their teachings to lead others to Christ. This is something a parishioner or his or her congregation may want to check out if hitting the streets with the gospel is a major priority.

Christian Coffeehouses (www.christiancoffeehouse.info/find.htm)

The focus in a coffeehouse is on entertainment and relaxation. Some people have trouble with the idea of entertainment being a part of ministry. However, the intention is that, at the end of the day or week, a person can simply go to a coffeehouse, be in a relaxed, laid-back atmosphere, hear live Christian music, and take it easy in a Christian environment. Most people dress casually, but they feel free to dress up, wear jeans or anything in between. A coffeehouse is also a good environment for bringing a nonbeliever to hear the gospel in a low-key, unthreatening environment.

Aftershock (www.youthexplosion.com)

Youth pastor Adam Durso from Christ Tabernacle Church in Queens, New York, created a ministry geared toward urban youths. On Friday nights, nearly 700 young people come to Aftershock to hear hip-hop praise and the word of God. Aftershock is the largest Christian youth group in New York City. They use DJs, guest rappers and videos that relate to the young people within the community. They have designed a concert-style event that attracts hundreds of youths from off the street. They also offer these young people Bible studies, where they talk about real issues.

Five Elements of Effectively Reaching Urban Youth

All of these different ministers possess some similarities. In order to reach the hip-hop generation, there are several things a person must remember. After identifying five elements each ministry must have if they hope to be effective in reaching the hip-hop generation, I will also suggest practical ways to implement these elements in the quest to reach hip-hoppers.

1. It is important for a church to develop a culture of evangelism.

Most churches are geared toward encouraging believers, and they often end up alienating nonbelievers. Do not forget, one of the purposes of the church is to reach nonbelievers. Because reaching people takes work and often makes non-Christians feel uncomfortable, many churches do not go out and try to evangelize as much as they should. The ministries who are effective in reaching this generation aggressively pursue nonbelievers instead of waiting for them to come to us. Remember, being passive will not get the church anywhere.

Practical Application: Church leaders might consider sponsoring an evangelism night once a month. Whether at a college campus, the local mall or other places young people hang out, this would be a good opportunity to reach out to the community. In addition, sponsoring a Christian hip-hop concert and other events geared toward youths or young adults is always a great way to attract them. Remember, a strategy is necessary to bring more young adults into church.

2. It is important to offer young people intimate settings.

Many effective ministries who reach the hip-hop generation offer intimate settings where youths can interact not only with other youths but also with mature Christians. Offering a roundtable-type discussion environment where young people can discuss important issues is critical. Young people do not always feel comfortable in a traditional church setting. Many young people need to feel connected. Additionally, this generation's attention span is short. Thus, sitting through lengthy messages is something most in this generation avoid.

Traditional church is often really impersonal and does not always meet people's needs. For example, people do not have an opportunity to raise their hand in the middle of a sermon to ask questions. That sounds bizarre, but there are many people who come to church who have questions about what they have heard. Churches should consider having a person at each service that people can approach if they have any questions, since many people walk out of church confused.

Practical Application: I like the idea of churches hosting "real talk" sessions instead of Bible studies for young adults. Remember that most nonbelievers will not come to a Bible study. Yet, there are some who will come to a real talk session, especially if the issues relate to them. A lively discussion will hold their attention and enable them to learn different Biblical principles that they can apply to their lives. In addition, an opportunity to share with the group makes them feel connected and wanted.

Finding strategies to make church more personal is one key to gaining and retaining more members of the hip-hop generation. This is especially true among men. Women tend to seek out interpersonal relationships, while men usually do not, so it is especially important that the church find ways to get men connected.

3. Make sure the gospel is presented in a practical and real way.

The gospel must be presented in a practical way so that young people can understand how the Bible relates to their lives. There are so many churches from Sunday to Sunday who teach the same old, tired messages. If what is coming out of the pulpit is not real and practical, this generation will tune it out. We live in an age where motivational speakers like Les Brown and Jim McCormick are taking Biblical principles and teaching them better than most pastors. However, they are not marketing the gospel in these motivating sessions. What they are marketing is success. Of course, everyone wants to be successful in life.

When someone walks through the doors of a church, the first thing that is on their mind is whether the experience will make their life more successful. Ultimately, this will determine whether they stay or go. While success is important, it is critical that the church makes sure they distinguish between success in the world and success in the kingdom of God. Sadly, I have met too many Christians who judge their success in life by the kind of car or home they own. Churches that are able to articulate godly success and help those in the church reach their goals have a leg up in developing a ministry that will keep young adults coming.

Practical Application: Churches should consider sponsoring sessions where they invite speakers in to talk about practical issues. For example, young people can benefit from seminars about how to build a business or ministry. Not only that, finding people in the church who can mentor them in the area they desire to focus on is a great idea. Many young people in the church have a passion to accomplish tasks for God, but they do not always have the necessary guidance and support. When young people see that a person is really serious about helping them reach their dreams, they will become more serious about helping the church members reach theirs.

4. Find creative ways to present the gospel.

Ministries that are effective in reaching the hip-hop generation understand how to be creative. Innovation is required to keep a young person's attention. There are tons of creative ways to present the gospel. Most churches are trapped in the mindset that the pastor has to preach for one hour each Sunday to have an effective service. However preaching is just one method of communicating the gospel. The more creative an environment the church can create, the more this generation will be interested in attending. Effective ministries geared to the hip-hop generation not only discover ways to be creative, but also implement them in their services.

Practical Application: Some people may respond to a dramatic presentation that portrays Biblical principles. What about showing a brief movie, after which the pastor discusses some principles from that movie? We live in a very high-tech world, where young people watch videos and DVDs. Showing videos is often a good idea for visual learners. Being creative sometimes involves looking at the available resources and brainstorming ways to utilize those resources to reach your community. Additionally, researching a community's interests is important. When designing a service for them, their input is vital.

5. This generation needs to see that we care.

This generation does not value church membership as past generations have. Twenty years ago, it was important for a Christian to be a part of a local church. Many of those people were committed to their church, through thick and thin. Those days are long gone. Nowadays, a parishioner really has to show people that he or she cares about them in order to keep them in church. More than any other group, it is important that the hip-hop generation knows that we care. Many of these young people have been hurt and have been in environments where people took advantage of them. If people care, it is going to be demonstrated in people's actions. Ultimately, caring is about giving of oneself, which is something the church needs to do more as a whole.

Practical Application: As young adults come into the church, it may be wise to assign a member to mentor them. This could be a person they can get to know and can go to when they have questions or concerns. Inviting some of these young people over for dinner or offering to hang out with them is often a good idea. Being willing to spend time with people and hearing their hopes, dreams and fears is always a good way to connect with others. Overall, creating a loving, safe environment where people can grow to develop trust not only in God, but also in the people around them, is tremendously important.

Chapter 5
Christian Hip-Hop 101

"Hip-hop is the hook that might draw them in, but what keeps them is building a relationship with God and with other people that are here."
— Urban D., pastor of Crossover Church

Christian Hip Hop 101

As I continue to talk about solutions, I will spend this chapter looking at Christian hip-hop. Christian hip-hop is similar to hip-hop, but its goal is to reach youths with the gospel of Jesus Christ. Over the years, this movement has been a controversial topic within the church. There are some who believe that hip-hop shouldn't be used by the church to help draw young people to Christ. Nevertheless, there are some within the church who are using the genre to impact this generation for Christ. To help you decide for yourself about Christian hip-hop, and to help readers develop an objective perspective about the genre, I will talk briefly about the artists, events and other helpful information necessary to uncover the best-kept secret in the music industry.

Christian Emcees

Not all Christian rappers rapping about Jesus are truly representing Christ. I thought I would make that clear up front. Take the example of Kanye West, who released a hit single entitled *Jesus Walks*. The difference between people like Kanye West and many other Christian emcees is whether they are using hip-hop to make a living or to reach youth for Christ. Kanye West, Mase Betha and other rappers never professed to be Christian emcees, nor does the Christian hip-hop community claim them.

Unfortunately, the church supports many artists like Kanye West. For example, I was disappointed in 2001 when so many within the church supported long-time secular rapper KRS ONE when he came out with a Christian album entitled "Spiritual Minded." I saw his album in many Christian bookstores across the country. There were even churches who invited him to minister, despite the fact that KRS ONE has believed and does believe that hip-hop is a religion, and that Jesus Christ is just one path of many to God.

I was overjoyed to see the Christian hip-hop community protest the Stellar Awards when they nominated Kanye West as Christian Hip-Hop Artist of the Year. The Christian hip-hop community did that because they did not want their genre to be associated with sin, sex, violence and the other things West promotes. Just because some churches may have tried to use West and others like him as a ministry tool, do not assume that the Christian hip-hop community supports these artists.

The genre has done more than slap the word "Christian" in front of "hip-hop." There really are some young people within the Christian hip-hop community who are just as passionate about God as Christians who do not participate in the hip-hop culture. The only difference is that those within the Christian hip-hop community dress and talk a little differently than the average Christian. These individuals might show up in church wearing jeans and a jersey instead of a suit and tie.

I wish I had the time to discuss all the Christian emcees that are using hip-hop strictly to represent God. Trust me, there are many artists who would be great to invite to minister at your church, or whose CD Christians should purchase. I will encourage anyone who may be concerned about supporting Christian hip-hop to take the time to do the proper research. What I am offering is a starting point. Looking up one of the following 20 ministries will illustrate what Christian emcees are all about.

Christian Hip-Hop Artists

ASON (www.bigsonny.com), **Cross Movement** (www.crossmovement.com), **Corey Red & Precise** (www.redprecise.

com), **Christcentric** (www.christcentric.net), **Damon Lamar** (www.damonlamar.com), **Frontlynaz** (www.frontlynaz.com), **Fros't** (www.fros-t.com), **GRITS** (www.grits7.com), **Hazakim** (www.hazakim.com), **Idol King** (www.idolking.org), **Knine** (www.kninemusic.com), **KJ 52** (www.kj52.com), **Platinum Soul** (www.platinumsoulsinc.com), **Richie Righteous** (www.richierighteous.com), **Redeemed Thought** (www.redeemedthought.com), **Sean Slaughter** (www.slaughtermusic.com), **Todd Bangz** (www.bangtheory.biz), **Timothy Brindle** (www.lampmode.com), **Tragedy** (www.sgrmusicgroup.com) and **Vocab Malone** (www.vocabmalone.com) are just 20 Christian emcees worth learning more about.

Events

Christian hip-hop events have come a long way. There was a time when it was hard to find an event featuring Christian emcees that had a quality sound system and artists who put on a good show. While Christian hip-hop is designed to minister to young people, concert promoters in the late 1990s started to realize that it is vital that Christian hip-hop concerts be excellent and entertaining. That is why it not uncommon to see flashy lights and well-decorated stages at such concerts. One of the primary goals of these concerts is to grab the attention of youths who normally would not attend church and keep them interested long enough to hear the gospel of Jesus.

One thing you should know about these concerts is that most of the events feature an altar call and ministry during the performance. At such times, Christian emcees usually stop the music and begin to minister the gospel to the youth who are in attendance. Sometimes the ambiance is reminiscent of church, except that an emcee is doing the ministering. What the Christian hip-hop community has done is to replace the choir with two turntables. In other words, instead of outreaches featuring choir music and organs, the Christian hip-hop community holds outreaches that feature Christian emcees and deejays.

There are numerous events that go on each week featuring Christian hip-hop artists. Many of these events are outreaches within different communities and concerts that local churches sponsor. Some parts of the country have more events than others. Cities like New York, Houston, Philadelphia and Atlanta seem to be constantly hosting Christian hip-hop events. However, cities like Denver, Kansas City, Phoenix and Washington, D. C., also have such events, although less often.

Many of the local events are not well promoted, and so a search may be necessary. It is important to find out who usually sponsors events in your area. Getting on their mailing list or contacting them will allow a person to get plugged in to what is going on. Tour schedules are also available at Christian hip-hop artists' Web sites.

Rap Fest is an annual event that is one of the oldest Christian hip-hop events around. Salem Coffee House in New York has been sponsoring this event for more than 10 years. The concert takes place on the second Saturday in August in the Bronx, New York. Each year, about 30 Christian emcees perform in an outdoor concert. This event has a "family reunion" feel as participants have the opportunity to meet and come together in fellowship with thousands of Christian hip-hop fans from around the country. For more information about this event, you can log onto www.rapfest2000.com.

The Holy Hip-Hop Awards take place in Atlanta during the Dr. Martin Luther King, Jr. holiday. This particular event features a showcase on Friday night and an awards show on Saturday. It gives fans an opportunity to see hundreds of artists from around the country and to come together in fellowship with other Christian hip-hop fans. Even though this affair features Christian artists from around the country, please be warned, there are many artists performing who have a southern style of rap. For more information about this event, log onto www.holyhiphop.com.

Each year, the Flavor Alliance and Crossover Community Church put on an event that speaks to the very core of what Christian hip-hop music is all about: ministry! Crossover

Community Church has become nationally known for its hip-hop ministry, which reaches hundreds of urban youths and adults. Each year, church leaders use this weekend to give people the tools they need to reach this generation for Christ. The weekend includes workshops, street outreaches, concerts and Crossover's regular hip-hop youth and adult services. In my view, this is the most complete Christian hip-hop event in the industry. For more about this event, log on to www.flavoralliance.com.

The Texas Holy Hip-Hop Achievement Awards is an annual event designed to honor those who have excelled in Christian hip-hop within the state of Texas. This is not only an awards show, but also a quality concert. The event usually takes place in June and features a nationwide array of artists. Even though most of those in attendance are from Texas, they gladly welcome people from all around the country. For more information about this event, log on to www.dasouth.com.

Christian Hip-Hop Over the Internet

The Christian hip-hop community started to utilize the World Wide Web in the early 1990s. I have personally followed Christian hip-hop Web sites for more than seven years now. One thing I have noticed is that it is difficult to keep one of these sites going. Speaking from my experience as the editor of an online Christian hip-hop magazine (www.wtwmagazine.com), most of these sites do not receive much support and end up folding after a couple of years. Consequently, most of the following sites are no longer around or are struggling to stay alive.

One of the first Web sites that featured Christian hip-hop was www.godzhouse.com. This site contained a heavy freestyle community and had some articles about Christian hip-hop. In the early 1990s, this was one of the primary places to come together in fellowship for the Christian hip-hop community. One Mind (www.om95.com) was another Christian hip-hop Web site that covered the genre in the mid 1990s. They were known for their honest music reviews. Most Christian hip-hop CDs were not high quality then, and One Mind did not have a problem writing music reviews that reflected this lack of quality. Neither of these Web sites is presently running.

One of the most popular Christian hip-hop sites of all time is www.hiphopzone.com. This site was launched in 1996. It reached its peak in the late 1990s as they featured interviews, covered events, and wrote stories about Christian hip-hop. This site set a standard for such websites. Yet, as years went by, the content and energy that was pumped into the site diminished. By 2000, this Web site became one big message board, as thousands of young people tuned in each day to post and find out what was going on within the Christian hip-hop community. Unfortunately, the board featured too many immature debates and believers. Currently, this site is trying to regroup.

Shereofhiphop.com (www.shereofhiphop.com) started in the late 1990s as well. The site is one of the few sites I have seen that started in the 1990s and has stood the test of time. This site has everything from music reviews, news, interviews, a message board and a store.

As we entered into the new millennium, there were several other sites that did a good job covering Christian hip-hop. Hiphopgateway.com (www.hiphopgateway.com) was a decent site that featured interviews, news and music reviews. They consistently put out content for about five years. They recently folded because of a lack of support and funds.

I started *What's The Word* magazine (www.wtwmagazine.com) in January 2000. This is an online magazine that puts out monthly editions designed to help young people gain a closer relationship with Jesus Christ. We also do interviews and write music reviews and articles. I am proud to say that, over the years, WTW magazine has been one of the most frequently updated and Christ-centered Christian hip-hop sites in the industry.

Dasouth.com (www.dasouth.com) was launched a couple years after *What's The Word*. Dasouth.com is a network of Christian hip-hop Web sites. Instead of many artists having their own Web sites, more than 20 Christian hip-hop artists came together in the spirit of unity to develop one big site. One of the highlights of this site is the Bus Stop (online store). In my view, this is the best place to go to purchase often times hard-to-find Christian hip-hop CDs.

Theyuinon.com (www.theyuinon.com) is another good site that is guided by a similar concept. They are a movement of people who are involved in Christian hip-hop. They come together in fellowship with each other and complete projects together. Their finest project was the HER Project that was released in 2004. This was a CD that featured six female emcees (Light, Sistah D, Mahogany, EP and Technique, and Shekinah) that dealt with real issues and struggles women deal with everyday.

Hiphopforthesoul.com (www.hiphopforsoul.com) is also a quality site to visit if you want to find out about Christian hip-hop. They do a really good job of keeping their site up-to-date and interesting. They also have one of the better online stores, where they offer a great selection of Christian hip-hop.

Rapzilla.com (www.rapzilla.com) has been around since 2003 and has a lot to offer as well. As a matter of fact, we awarded them the 2005 Web Site of the Year Award for their hard work. There are many links and videos on this site.

Feed Magazine is the best print Christian hip-hop magazine in the industry. To find out more about this magazine, log on to www.feedstop.com.

To buy Christian hip-hop CDs, first check the artist's Web site. There are plenty of other places to find Christian hip-hop over the Internet. Five of my personal favorites are:

- www.neworldmusic.net
- www.jydist.com
- www.subculturemerch.com/store/hhfts/index.asp
- www.flavoralliance.com/hhs2.html
- www.buyholyhiphop.net

Chapter 6

Action Plan

"Hope begins in the dark – the stubborn hope that if you just show up and try to do the right thing, the dawn will come. You wait and watch and work; You don't give up."

- Anne Lamott

I am assuming that readers purchased this book to learn how to reach the hip-hop generation with the gospel of Jesus Christ. The hip-hop generation is not someone else's problem. It is only when we take ownership of something that we make progress in applying solutions. This is a crisis that affects us all. One can only imagine the kind of world the next generation will grow up to create if this nation continues down its present path. That predicament will not disappear as a result of prayer. It is time for us all to take action.

Throughout this book, it was my goal to provide practical solutions regarding how to reach the hip-hop generation for Jesus. Now it is time for readers to establish some goals as well. Whether by becoming a better parent or by sponsoring an outreach, it is important that action be taken. Action is the only thing that will get many of these young people off the street and into the church. Action is the only thing that will change the tide of immorality in this country.

I want to close with a couple of testimonies. These are members of the hip-hop generation who turned their backs on God. Yet, God changed their lives because someone used some of the methods I suggested in this book. There are million of young people, just like these you are about to read about, who have not been reached yet. The question is, is the church going to do what it takes to reach them? Remember, there is nothing wrong with the word of God; it is just the church that has problems. Let's work together to turn this generation from a lost generation to a chosen one (1 Peter 2:9).

Wanda

"I actually grew up in the church. When I was a child, I hated my parents because they didn't allow me to do anything fun. I remember being 17 years old, and I could not have phone calls from the opposite sex, wear makeup, or stay out past 9:30 p.m. While my friends were out having a good time at different social functions, I was either at home or at a church. I felt like I spent my childhood being punished. I always thought church was boring. The best thing I enjoyed about church was leaving and meeting a couple of young people who experienced the same struggles as me.

"As I've gotten older, I've had an opportunity to leave home and go to college. In this process, I did not make too many wise choices. Being rebellious, I had sex with four or five different guys the first semester in school. I also experimented with drugs and alcohol. The more I sank in sin, the less I thought about going to church. As a matter of fact, more than five years went by and I can count on one hand the number of times I had been to the house of God. One day, I received an invitation to a women-only discussion about relationships between men and women at a local church. I was interested in going only because I had just been dumped by a guy who was simply using me. In general, I was tired of the life I was living and wanted something different.

"At the meeting, it just seemed as if God was talking directly to me, as I realized that I was making a huge mistake with my life when I was not living for God. For years, I was searching for the love that only God could give me. That night, I invited Jesus Christ back into my life and have been living for Him ever since. Over time, I have learned to forgive myself for all the things I have done wrong, after realizing that God had forgiven me. I now desire to one day help women who are in the same position I was in."

Andrew

"I grew up in the streets. I used to be that brother many church members walked past in fear because they thought I was going to rob them. The streets were the only thing I knew. I personally never knew too many people who went to church. I always thought church was a waste of time and full of hypocrites. Yet, there were a couple of times that I wished I was in church. This occurred especially during those moments when it seemed as if my life was on the line. I witnessed almost all my boys die, and I knew it was just a matter of time for me.

"I remember walking past a concert in my neighborhood on a hot summer day. It was a group on stage, rapping, so I decided to stay for a moment to check the concert out. When I found out they were rapping about Jesus, I wanted to leave. Yet, there was something inside of me that would not let me go. I stayed until the end, as one of the emcees gave an altar call. At that point, I thought about my life and the direction I was headed. For the first time in my life, I realized I had a one-way ticket to Hell if I did not give my heart to Christ.

"My life has not been the same since that day. Two years later, I found myself helping out with the youth in my church, and reaching out to people in my community who were in the same lifestyle I was in. I appreciate my pastor because he respects my advice on how to reach youth. I believe that urban gospel music is the best tool for reaching young people in the streets. I just hope the church wakes up and starts using it."

Bonus Section #1

The History of Christian Hip Hop

Pioneers

By most accounts, Christian hip-hop began somewhere in early 1980s. There is no way to know who was actually the first Christian emcee. Honestly, I have heard a ton of names proposed. At the very least, we know the genre first became public in the early- to mid-1980s – mainly in Nashville, Tennessee (Christian music's capital) and through the Los Angeles underground. With national distribution through Nashville-based companies like Broken Records, Brainstorm Artists International and Word Records Limited, Christian hip-hop was exposed to Christian markets around the country.

Even though no one really knows for sure who the original Christian rappers were, most credit artists like M.C. Sweets, JC & the Boyz, Michael Peace and Stephen Whiley with being some of the first to represent Christ on the microphone. In the early 1980s, there were only a handful of Christian emcees releasing albums. These emcees mostly performed on street corners, ciphers and at evangelist outreaches.

The early years of Christian hip-hop were a rough time for many Christian emcees. The world did not accept the genre, nor did the church. Many pastors refused to support Christian hip-hop and could not understand why Christians would use something so negative to reach youths. It was common for those within the genre to be rebuked by church leaders for mixing hip-hop and Christianity. There were some Believers who even thought that Christian hip-hop was of the Devil.

Keep in mind, this was during a time when secular hip-hop went commercial, as groups like RUN DMC and Kurtis Blow began to birth the hip-hop generation. Even though Christian hip-hop lacked quality back then, it seemed to some people to be the ideal tool for reaching youths as Christians started rapping. On many occasions, without the aid of a sound system or other devices utilized by artists today, many of these emcees rapped about Jesus in local parks, community centers or wherever there was an audience.

Christian hip-hop was not perfect during this time. There were Christian emcees involving themselves in "battling." When emcees battled, they would put each other down while rapping. Battling was common in hip-hop, especially in the 1980s, as artists would try to gain notoriety by verbally bashing other emcees in the industry. Many times, this would lead to groups of emcees "beefing." There were Christian emcees who attempted to bring that same competitive spirit into Christian hip-hop. Nevertheless, this and other problems never overshadowed what God wanted to do with the genre.

The earlier Christian emcees did not always put out albums as frequently as artists do today. It was common for an emcee to have been rapping for years and not release a project. Nevertheless, that time period did produce a couple of memorable releases. Stephen Wiley was one of the first emcees to have a commercial release and a distributed gospel rap cassette in 1985, called "Bible Break." This particular album was played in many Sunday schools across America.

Even though Stephen Wiley was one of the first to release a commercial album, Michael Peace and others were producing music during this time, as well. Michael Peace released "Rock It Right" in 1987. Both of these gentlemen and others had the opportunity to travel across the country, rapping for Jesus. Even though there were those against Christian hip-hop, there were many who became supporters and saw the need for Christian hip-hop after experiencing artists like Wiley and Peace.

There were many other Christian emcees making music during this time as well. One of the first females in Christian rap music,

MC Ge Gee, was born in the Bronx and raised in Dallas, where her parents ran an inner-city youth outreach. In fact, their ministry was the subject of the film *The Cross and the Switchblade*. She was not a hardcore or pop rapper. Instead, she picked up the serious, issue-oriented street-poetry legacy of her late brother, D-Boy. She ended up releasing an album entitled "And Now the Mission Continues" in January 1991.

MC Ge Gee's brother, D-Boy, is considered the first Christian hip-hop martyr. Gang members shot him to death in his community in 1991. He was killed in a community that was not only full of gang activity, but was also the place he was trying to win over for Christ. Before he died, he managed to leave behind some music. His album, "Peace 2 the Poet," was a quality release that offered his listeners some powerful, Christ-centered lyrics. In many ways, D-Boy represented the commitment many artists had during this time, as he was willing to die rather than quit preaching the gospel in a dangerous community.

DC Talk was also an early pioneer of the genre, but its members had a more pop sound. This Christian rock band formed in the late 1980s. They began as a hip-hop act, but in the mid-1990s they reinvented themselves as a pop/rock group. In both instances, they found immense critical and commercial success in both the Christian music industry and the general market.

Before they changed to pop/rock, DC Talk was one of the first groups to bring some notoriety to Christian hip-hop, as they were the first to obtain major distribution within the Christian market. In 1989, they released their self-titled debut album on Forefront Records. They gained some crossover success when their *Heavenbound* music video received airplay on BET. Their follow-up album, "Nu Thang" (1990), also received attention for its hip-hop/pop styling, which reminded people of artists like M.C. Hammer and the Fresh Prince.

A crew called Freedom of Soul also dropped several projects during this time period that helped lay the foundation for the genre.

Some of their projects include "Caught In A Land of Time" and "The Second Comin'." These and other projects made them one of the more popular groups during that time. There were also groups from the West Coast, like Idol King, LPG and the S.F.C. (Soldiers for Christ) crew.

Christian hip-hop fans might remember the name Soldiers For Christ because this was the crew that Soup the Chemist came from (an emcee who went on to release numerous albums, as well, through the 1990s). The Idol King remained in the genre as well; they released an album entitled "Not By Power" in 2004. LPG helped to start the Tunnel Rats, who ended up being a popular crew in the late 1980s.

Some of the other pioneers during this period are wA-1 Swift, a husband and wife team famous for rapping on one of Kirk Franklin's albums in the mid 1990s. E.T.W. released several albums during this period as well. Their first album, entitled "End Time Warriors," was released in 1989. Another pioneer in Christian hip-hop was The Twelfth Tribe. They released their first album in 1991, entitled "Knowledge Is the Tree of Life." Preachas in the Hood, once on the Grapetree label, did a lot of street ministry as he rocked the microphone for Christ during this era as well.

Other Christian emcees in the 1980s were Str8 Young Gangstaz, Positive D, Lady J, D.O.C. and Transformation Crusade. There are actually hundreds of others who populated the Christian hip-hop community in the 1980s. These and other emcees went on to birth the beginning of Christian hip-hop. As Christian hip-hop left the 1980s and entered the 1990s, a strong foundation was built, as more Christian emcees began to release quality music.

Christian Hip Hop in 1990s

As the genre entered the early 1990s, the music industry suddenly witnessed a growing number of Christian emcees. As the emcees grew, so did the number of albums. Yet, Christian hip-hop still did not receive much attention in the music industry during this period. One of the reasons why it was difficult for many fans to get their hands on the music was because many artists were forced to sell their albums mostly after concerts. Nevertheless, for the first time Christian hip-hop albums were consistently being sold across the country.

The music was being sold in select stores. Until recently, and with few exceptions, a person could only obtain Christian rap by going to Christian bookstores; these tend to be in the suburbs. Consequently, many urban youths were not exposed to the music. This was one of things that slowed the genre from catching on across the country. One thing that helped Christian hip-hop during that time was the Internet. For the first time, people in the industry could connect with one another across the country. Fans could go online to read about and purchase music. The Internet helped to expand the Christian hip-hop community. Two of the first Web sites geared to promote Christian hip-hop were www.godzhouse.com and www.om95.com.

During the mid 1990s, Christian hip-hop started to produce their first nationwide artists. Emcees like T-bone, Gospel Gangsters and Dynamic Twins obtained nationwide recognition as they released albums and traveled across the nation doing shows. T-Bone's career began in 1991 with the JC Crew. He was one of the key emcees during this period who won respect on the street, while his bold testimony won him respect in the church. "Redeemed Hoodlum," his debut album, was issued in 1993, and "Tha Life of a Hoodlum," which followed in 1995, made him a star. He is still releasing albums today and traveling across the country doing shows.

Rappers Noel and Robbie Arthur, known as The Dynamic Twins, released their first album in 1991, entitled "Word 2 The Wize." These twins from California traveled around the country, ministering to thousands of youths and helping to put Christian hip-hop on the map. They not only released several quality albums, but made appearances on albums from fellow West Coast rappers like JC And The Boyz, Chuckie P and SFC.

The Gospel Gangsters were another popular group during this time. They had a ministry directly to the gang community, as they brought a hardcore, West Coast style to Christian hip-hop. They have had numerous albums and have performed shows all over the world. One of their better albums was entitled "The Exodus." This project and others established the Gospel Gangsters as one of the premier Christian hip-hop groups during the 1990s. They later changed their name to Camp 8, and are now working with professional basketball player Alan Houston to continue to release music.

GRITS was formed in 1993. Eventually signing with Gotee Records, the duo dropped their rookie album in 1995, and followed it with "Factors of Seven" two years later. GRITS scored a major national breakthrough with the 1999 project "Grammatical Revolution." Among other accolades, the album earned the group a Billboard Video Award and an appearance on the nationally syndicated radio show *Sway & Tech*. Over the years, GRITS has been one of Christian hip-hop's best-selling groups, as they are one of the few groups to have sold more than 100,000 units.

Grapetree Records was the leading Christian hip-hop label in the 1990s, releasing more than 20 albums. The CEO of Grapetree, Knolly Williams, used gangsta rap to deliver a positive Christian message when he started the label in 1993. Grapetree Records was made up of former dope dealers, gangstas, hustlers and thugs who had turned away from their lives of crime. Artists like Prime Minister, LG Wise and Nuwine made Grapetree Records famous and helped this Texas-based label reach thousands of young people.

In 1998, the label reported sales topping $2 million. Their best-selling releases have been the series of "Heaven's Hip-Hop" and "Muzik to Ride" compilations – each selling in the 10,000- to 30,000-unit range. The label later broke up. Many of the former Grapetree artists are still ministering across the country today. To date, Grapetree has been one of the most successful Christian hip-hop record labels in the genre's history.

Although Christian hip-hop continued to expand in the mid-1990s, the genre seemed to be stagnating, as the music received little airplay on most major radio stations across the country. This was partly because of the lack of quality. Inundated with simple beats and slow rhymes, Christian hip-hop could not keep up with what was being produced in secular hip-hop. This turned off many potential fans and kept Christian hip-hop from achieving any kind of commercial success.

In the late 1990s, the genre took a turn for the better as The Cross Movement released "House of Representatives." This particular project was the first Christian hip-hop album to live up to the standard of excellence hip-hop fans normally experience in the secular community as far as production, lyrics and presentation. Christian hip-hop now had a higher standard to live up to, as this project made The Cross Movement stars in the industry.

The Cross Movement, based in Philadelphia, went on to be featured in national media outlets, including *The Washington Post*, *The Source Magazine* and *Time Magazine*. *Time Magazine* found The Cross Movement's lyrics to be so compelling that they referred to the Ambassador's rap, *Blood Spilla*, as the voice to educate America on the new pop music. *The Source Magazine*, known in the entertainment industry as THE magazine of the hip-hop culture, focused on The Cross Movement for their 2001 Christian rap feature, *God Is On the Mic*.

Other groundbreaking albums in the late 1990s included "The Mark of the East" compilation and "Christology: In Layman's Terms." "The Mark of the East" compilation was released in the summer of 1999 and featured some of the finest Christian hip-hop artists from New York. This CD gave us classics like *Six Million Ways* and *It's My Turn*. "Christology: In Layman's Terms" is considered by many to be the best Christian hip-hop solo project ever produced, and it helped make the Ambassador a nationwide star.

Throughout the years, DJ MAJ has been one of the top Christian hip-hop deejays as he toured with artists like Kirk

Franklin and Toby Mac. DJ MAJ has released several quality mix tapes, starting with his first in 1997, entitled "Sabbatical Transit." His best album was "Full Plates" (2001). In my view, this is one of the best Christian hip-hop mix tapes ever. In addition, during the late 1990s, a group called The Tunnel Rats sparked much debate within the industry. They and others groups drew many critics for not making Christ-centered music. Despite the controversy, New Breed, part of the Tunnel Rats and a brother and sister team, released several quality projects during this time. They established themselves as one of the best groups within Christian hip-hop when they released "Stop The Music" in 2003.

Speaking of deejays, there have been many Christian radio disco jockeys over the years. Floyd Cray was one of the first. In 1995, he formed the radio show *Gospel Vibrations*. In addition, in 1997, *Gospel Vibrations* music reviews was started and featured as a CD review column for the *Tri-State Voice Christian Newspaper*. Later in that same year, Cray thought of a way to bring Christian music videos to cable, and *Gospel Vibrations Video Music Show* kicked off on public access in the New York Metro area. His show is aired on 89.1 WFDU-FM every Saturday morning, from 1:15 a.m. to 6 a.m.

The Christian hip-hop community also has seen many good producers of the years. One of the more notable has been Lee Jerkins. He has produced Cross Movement, Out of Eden, Corey Red and Precise, Monique Walker and others around the industry. He later developed a Christian entertainment company called Rocksoul Entertainment. Sister Dee, Shai Linne, J Silas and Michelle Bonilla were once signed to his record company and featured on the "Rocksoul Entertainment Compilation." This album featured various artists from around the industry.

The 1990s would not be complete if we did not mention B.B. Jay. He was the first Christian emcee to sign with a major record label – Jive Records. His debut album, "Universal Concussion," was a quality album, but he could never develop a strong following because he was considered too holy for the world, but too secular for the church. So, after just one album, he was released from his contract and is now looking to release independent albums under his own label, JizFat Records.

Overall, Christian hip-hop made some progress during the 1990s, and many churches began to support the genre. The community grew as the genre saw emcees from all around the country representing Christ on the microphone. Christian hip-hop was now a respectable genre as the quality of the music increased.

Christian Hip-Hop in the 2000s

Even though the quality of Christian hip-hop rose to another level during the 1990s, the genre was still struggling to gain commercial success. The average Christian hip-hop artists were still selling fewer than 5,000 units per project during this period. Meanwhile, the genre's secular counterparts were selling million of albums per project, and influencing young people around the world.

Still, progress had been made, as artists like Corey Red & Precise and Da' T.R.U.T.H. gained nationwide distribution for their albums. Da' T.R.U.T.H.'s first solo project, "The Moment of Truth," made some "noise" on the *Billboard* chart and was one of the most successful Christian hip-hop albums in this decade, as far the number of units it pushed. Corey Red & Precise thrilled fans across the country as they released their long-awaited album, "Resistance Iz Futile." This project was one of the most anticipated projects ever. The two emcees from New York released several quality mix tapes that generated a lot of excitement for this ministry.

In the 2000s, Christian hip-hop became more explicit, not only in the types of issues Christian emcees talked about, but also in the way they talked about those issues. In the 1990s, the Christian hip-hop community was producing music that was geared more for the church, but now the Christian hip-hop community talked more about reaching young people in the streets. Artists like Japhia Life,

Solomon and Sean Slaughter were just a few artists who began to develop Christian rap for the streets. Their lyrics often times addressed real issues that are not commonly discussed in church.

Additionally, during this period, some artists started to make mix tapes to hand out to unsaved young people. A mix tape is an easy and cheap way for artists to get their music out to the general public. However, these mix tapes were controversial because many Christian hip-hop artists began to rap over secular beats they had no permission to use. After a couple of years of the market being saturated with them, this fad slowly died down.

Two key artists during this time were Urban D. and KJ 52. Urban D. is the pastor of the pioneering hip-hop Crossover Community Church in Tampa, Florida. His church has been a model for those who want to use hip-hop to reach youths. During this period, KJ 52 became one of the most recognizable Christian emcees out today. He won the 2004 Dove Award for Rap/Hip-Hop Album of the Year (for "It's Pronounced Five-Two") and received a 2005 Dove Award nomination for Rap/Hip-Hop Recorded Song of the Year (for *Back in the Day*) and for Rap/Hip-Hop Album of the Year (for "Soul Purpose"). He was best known for a song he wrote, *Dear Slim*, which is a letter he wrote to rapper Eminem.

One of the best cities for Christian hip-hop has been Houston. Led by Tre 9, this city has been a model for the rest of the Christian hip-hop community. In addition to the Texas Achievement Awards, they also have a unity and love for each other that is often times unmatched. Many of these artists teamed up to build Dasouth.com, a Web site community that features numerous ministries. Former Cross Movement member Enock ended up moving to Houston and released his first solo album that made a lot "waves" in the industry. Along with him, Mark J, Cy and others helped Much Luvv Records become one of the top record labels in the industry.

Christian hip-hop has also broken into international markets as well. Fresh I.E. from Canada was nominated at the 46th Grammy

Awards for Best Gospel Rock Album. He was one of the first Christian hip-hop artists to achieve this honor. He is not the only Christian emcee from outside the U.S. Chris Greenwood, AKA Manafest, is a Toronto-bred hip-hop artist who has released several quality projects. Promise D'Apostle, also from Canada, released an album entitled "What I Know Is The Truth." His sophomore album, entitled "The Promise That Heaven Kept," came two years later and demonstrates his exceptional skills as a hip-hop artist.

Of course, we cannot forget about the ladies. There are several women who have made an impact for Christ using hip-hop during this period. Elle R.O.C., a female rap artist, earned a name for herself as a solo artist with multiple performances throughout the United States and abroad. She released "I Die Daily" several years ago, featuring songs that range from mellow, unfeigned ballads to audacious verbal admonishments that dare us not to dance, but represent Christ at the same time.

Tragedy, AKA La Toya Burns, has signed with Houston's Southern Gospeltality label. This inspirational MC got her start as a teen, performing on Houston's 97.9 KBXX, FM's "Roll Call," a sort of call-in talent contest on the station's morning show. She reigned from the latter part of 1994 to 1996, winning local acclaim and the attention of J-Dub, a production team at P. Diddy's Bad Boy Records. After dedicating her heart to Christ, she decided that secular music was not for her, and later became one of the better female Christian emcees in the industry as she released her first album, "Diamond in the Rough," in 2002.

Arguably the best female album ever released was the "HER Project." This was a project that featured six female emcees (Light, Sistah D, Mahogany, EP and Technique, and Shekinah) and dealt with real issues and struggles that women face every day. This was a well-produced project that ended up being a groundbreaking album, as women across the country experienced healing because of the ministry that came from the album.

Several emcees have come out of the secular community to become Christian emcees. Mr. Del is one. As a member of 3 6

Mafia, Mr. Del was enjoying the success of his first hit single with more than 500,000 copies sold. During Easter 2000, he discovered that God had a higher calling for his life and a greater purpose for his music. Three days after accepting Christ, Mr. Del completed "Enter the Light," his first Christian hip-hop release. Since then, he has become the founder and senior pastor of The City of Refuge Church and he heads up a team of rappers known as the Holy South Soldiers.

Other secular rappers turned Christian include Cheryl "Salt" James and Christopher "Play" Martin. Many of you probably first heard that Salt converted to Christianity when Kirk Franklin released the hit single *Stomp*. Back in the late 1980s, hip-hop was on its way to becoming a male-dominated art form, which is what made the emergence of Salt 'n' Pepa so significant. As the first all-female rap crew of importance (even their DJs were women), the group broke down a number of doors for women in hip-hop. James is now set to release an album entitled "Salt of the Earth."

Play, of the rap duo Kid 'n' Play, had a taste of success with several chart-topping singles. Kid 'n' Play did their part to make hip-hop more accessible with efforts like "Ain't Gonna Hurt Nobody" and "Rollin' With Kid 'n' Play," coordinated dance moves, and the successful *House Party* movie series. After overcoming several financial and legal problems, Christopher Martin currently serves as CEO of HP4 Digital Works (www.hp4digitalworks.com). He is also attempting to release some music and is working on a Christian hip-hop movie that should be released sometime in 2006.

Frankie Cutlass used to be a big-time New York DJ before he gave his heart to Christ. He worked with secular artists like Method Man, Big Daddy Kane and other big names in the hip-hop industry. He released one of the best mix tapes ever, featuring Corey Red, Todd Bangz and Street Discipline. Unfortunately, about a year after this album was released, Street Discipline went home to be with Jesus. Because of his untimely death, the world never got the opportunity to experience his gift to the fullest.

There have also been a couple of children grabbing the microphone for Christ. Lil iROCC Williams' major label debut came at the age of 13. As a freshman on the music scene, Lil iROCC achieved historical success with his self-titled debut CD in 2003 on EMI CMG. The CD made it to no. 15 on the Sound Scan Christian Album Charts and to no. 27 on the Top Contemporary Christian Albums Charts, along with no. 33 on the Gospel Albums Charts. Lil J Xavier from Texas was also only about 12 or 13 years old when he started making waves in the industry. He released an album in 2003 entitled "I Got Be Me."

The world has seen more than 20 years of history from the Christian hip-hop community. There have been a lot of ups and downs but, most importantly, the Christian hip-hop community has reached thousands of young people for Christ. What can we expect from the next 20 years? Here are a couple of questions to ponder. Will the Christian hip-hop community ever see a Christian hip-hop artist go platinum? Will the Christian hip-hop community ever gain the influence that the secular hip-hop community has? Will the church ever fully embrace Christian hip-hop?

Bonus Section #2

What Awards: Honoring the Best in Christian Hip-Hop in 2005

Every year, *What's The Word* magazine honors the best in Christian hip-hop with the What Awards. These are individuals who worked hard in 2005 to advance the kingdom of God using Christian hip-hop. We simply want to give honor where honor is due. With no further ado, here is our list.

Group of the Year: Corey Red & Precise

Why: In 2004, they put out one of the hottest albums in the industry and went around the country ministering to thousands of young people. During this time, they established a high standard, not only with the quality of music they released, but also with the level of ministry each track contains. In 2005, after more than five years of ministry together, this duo from New York went their separate ways. Precise is now releasing a solo project on the Yuinon record label, and Corey Red is releasing a project on the Life Music label. We wanted to honor them with this award for their years of hard work within the industry.

Artists of The Year: Da' T.R.U.T.H.

Why: His debut album established this emcee from Philadelphia as one of the more notable artists in the industry. He also demonstrated that he could push units as he made some "noise" on the *Billboard* charts with "The Moment Of Truth." As The Cross Movement's first protégé, Da' T.R.U.T.H. has been using hip-hop as a tool to deliver the gospel since 1995. In 2004, he saw his official coming-out party, and in 2005 he came back strong with his second offering, entitled "The Faith." "The Faith" debuted at #7 on the Billboard Gospel Chart. This project continued to establish him as one of the premier artists in the industry as he traveled around the country, impacting many young people's lives for Christ.

Record Label of the Year: Cross Movement Records

Why: The Christian hip-hop community is still struggling to produce some quality record labels that offer Christian emcees quality distribution deals. There are a couple of very good ones, but one really stood out this year. We are talking about Cross Movement records. This label, based out of New Jersey, not only produced the most albums in 2005, but also some of the best. Phanatik, the Ambassador and TRU Life all released solo projects under this label in 2005. This label also released about four other albums (Lacrae's "Real Talk," Da' T.R.U.T.H.'s "The Faith," Flame's "Rewind" and J.R.'s "Metamorphosis") that hit the market this year.

Website of the Year: Rapzilla

Why: As I surf the Internet, the biggest problem I have witnessed among Christian hip-hop Web sites is that they are not often updated. There are only a couple sites that are updated frequently, and which provide people with quality information about Christian hip-hop. This is not the only thing we looked for when deciding on this award, but up-to-date information is important. Having said that, we give this award to Rapzilla. Many people appreciate the effort they put into this site. In addition, they came up with the first-ever Christian hip-hop tool bar (www.rapzilla.com/toolbar.htm). With this, one can stay connected to what is going on in the Christian hip-hop community.

Single of the Year: We Worship You

Why: It was clear after the Ambassador obtained his master's degree in theology that he was ready to teach the world a lot more about Christ and worship. His song about honoring God was the best song on the finest album in 2005. He used this particular song to teach his audience that Jesus Christ is worthy of our worship. The track also got plenty of spins around the country on many radio stations. This song characterizes everything we look for in a single. Christian hip-hop is not all about jumping up and down for Jesus. There are some times God wants His people to use hip-hop to worship Him.

Event of the Year: Texas Holy Hip-Hop Awards

Why: This annual event is designed to honor those who have excelled in Christian hip-hop in the state of Texas. The Texas Holy Hip-Hop Awards feature worships, an awards show and a great time of fellowship with Christian hip-hop supporters from around the country. We gave this event the award because it is a quality event, and because we want to encourage more states and cities to do what Texas is doing. How many cities work together to impact their community for Christ? This event is always produced excellently. This year's show featured artists like B.B. Jay, Lil Raskull and other nationwide artists.

New Artist of the Year: This'L

Why: There were many good candidates for New Artist of the Year in 2005. The Christian hip-hop community produces many new quality artists every year. In a very close race, This'L got the nod. Why? He not only released one of the better albums when he dropped "This House I Still Live," but also has made a name for himself throughout the industry with this project. Very few new artists made the impact that This'L did in 2005. This artist from St. Louis should be around for years to come, impacting lives for Christ.

Album of the Year: "Thesis"

Why: This project was not as good as Ambassador's first solo album, "Christology: In Laymen's Terms." Still, there were not many albums better than his first release. The Ambassador did not disappoint too many fans with his long-awaited second solo project. "The Thesis" was a well-produced album that had some incredible lyrics. This project will probably end up being the top-selling album in 2005 and impacting many young people's lives for Christ.

Person of the Year: Tonic

Why: This was the year that the Christian hip-hop community saw three solo albums from the Cross Movement. Plus, we witnessed albums from Da' T.R.U.T.H. and Flame, as well as several other albums that Cross Movement records released. As president of this record label, Tonic had his hand in all these projects. This was an outstanding year for him, especially since in 2004 he was at home, sick in bed. He came back in a huge way and helped released almost 10 quality albums off their label in one year. Tonic did a wonderful job saturating the market with some quality Christian hip-hop.

Lifetime Achievement Award: Michael Peace

Why: He was one of the first Christian emcees to release music, back in the mid-1980s. He traveled around the country, using Christian hip-hop in the face of adversity. Through it all, he helped lay a solid foundation for the genre we see today. Michael Peace is one of the few Christian hip-hop pioneers who is still around, helping this movement. He is no longer rapping but he is helping to mentor another generation of emcees and is still working with young people in Buffalo, New York.

Bonus Section #3

Top Ten Greatest Christian Hip-Hop Albums

There have been many quality Christian hip-hop albums over the years. I have taken the liberty of listing the albums I feel are the top 10 greatest Christian hip-hop albums of all times. I believe these 10 albums have been the best over the years as far as quality, ministry and how each has helped to shape this industry.

1. "House of Representatives" – Cross Movement (1999). We rated this as the best Christian hip-hop album of all time because production, lyrics and presentation-wise, this project helped take Christian hip-hop to another level. For all practical purposes, this project was the first Christian hip-hop CD that had the same level of quality as albums in the secular community. Every single song on this particular project had fans constantly pushing their repeat button. With tracks like *I Am That I Am*, *Think On These Things* and *Cypha' The Next Day*, this album provided many Christian hip-hop supporters with hours of enjoyment and ministry.

2. "Mark of the East" compilation – Various Artists (1999). This project featured artists like Corey Red, Precise, ADF and many other quality emcees from New York. This CD is for East Coast hardcore hip-hop fans. One of the special things about this particular project is that it broke the stereotype that Christians are soft and out of touch. This CD dealt with real issues that people from the streets struggle with every day. This project also gave us classic tracks like *Six Million Ways* and *It's My Turn*. Overall, this project helped set a standard throughout the industry and launched the careers of artists like Corey Red & Precise and ADF.

3. "Christology: In Laymen's Terms" – Ambassador (1999). In my view, this is the best solo Christian hip-hop album ever released. This album propelled the Ambassador to the top as one of the most-recognized and respected emcees in the industry. This project had everything a person would ever want in an album and more. This album was a classic, containing crafty lyrics, excellent production and interludes. Tracks like *Honor And Glory*, *Psalm 23* and *Hold Your Ground* made this particular project difficult to keep off our list.

    4. **"Factors of the Seven"** – GRITS (1997). GRITS was fresh off of their first record, "Mental Releases," which drew little attention from the Christian industry. However, hard work, combined with many talented producers, created a record light years ahead of their previous effort. Back in 1997, GRITS proved to be a group ahead of their time when they released "Factors of the Seven." This album enabled GRITS to become one of the top-selling Christian hip-hop groups of all time.

    5. **"Full Plates"** – DJ MAJ (2001). One of the special things about this album was the collection of artists on this project. Everyone from Pigeon John, Tunnel Rats and Minister Zion did a track on this album. With just under 20 tracks all expertly mixed, with scratches and cuts, this project is the best Christian hip-hop mix tape ever. This particular project produced classics singles like *What's My Name*, *Deceptions* and *7 Factors*. This album also made New Breed stars in the industry. Not bad for one mix tape.

    6. **"Heavenbound"** - DC Talk (1990). This album is the oldest album that made our list. This project, in particular, was a wonderful blend of grunge rock, rap, melodic pop and funk. During the early 1990s, this was not only one of the better albums, but also one of the most popular. This project is one of the first Christian hip-hop albums to gain a high level of commercial success throughout the gospel music industry. This project and others by DC Talk helped to put Christian hip-hop on the map during the 1990s.

    7. **"Tha Life of a Hoodlum"** – T-Bone (1995). This was T-Bone's second album. "Tha Life of a Hoodlum" features T-Bone's energetic flows over funky down-tempo beats and hooks. Some of

the better songs on this projected included *Amen Somebody*, *Drunk In The Spirit*, *Pushin' Up Daisies* and *Still Jabbin'*. T-Bone ended up doing his best work on this project. This CD also gave him one of the best names around the industry, and made him an ambassador for Christian hip-hop over the years.

8. "I Can See Clearly Now" - Gospel Gangstaz (1999). This was the Gospel Gangstaz's best project. This album has the most non-Christian sounds ever on a Christian rap album, and yet it still has biblically sound lyrics. This group from the West Coast was one of the first groups that made Christian hip-hop for young people in the streets. Believe me when I say that this group and album is not for everyone. They often push the line of decency in order to reach their audience at times.

9. "Resistance Iz Futile" – Corey Red & Precise (2004). This album was one of the most anticipated Christian hip-hop albums of all time. Ever since appearing on the "Mark of East" compilation in 1999, this duo from New York has been highly respected throughout the industry. When they released this project, no one lost respect for these two emcees as they delivered the best album out that particular year. With tracks like *What's Goin' On?*, *Da Matrix Joint* and *Christ Out*, this particular project has plenty to offer.

10. "City of Pain" – Mark J (2003). On this album, New York emcee Mark J takes his ministry to another level after having been in the industry for a number of years. This was one of the better albums I have heard in the last couple of years. This project was also the most diverse album I have listened to, including everything from rock to reggae to hip-hop. The single *National Anthem* was the best track on this album as it was a powerful battle cry for holy hip-hop, featuring some heavy beats and a hard vibe contrasted with serene choral hooks. Overall, this album was a pleasant surprise to many.

Bonus Section #4:

Q&A Session on Christian Hip-Hop

In an effort to help you understand the Christian hip-hop movement, I took a moment to respond to some of the claims a pastor launched against Christian hip-hop. This particular pastor's name is G. Craige Lewis. His website is located at www.exministries.com. Prayerfully, this section answers some of your questions about the genre and its validity.

Why choose to blame hip-hop and not the Devil for the condition of this generation?

1. G. Craige Lewis said: *"Hip-hop is not music! It is not a genre; it is not a specific sound or art form. Hip-hop is not rap either, but it is a religion/culture or a belief system that was birthed out of a desire to manifest one's self in a society that was deemed unfair to African-American's in the early 1970s…... Hip-hop has turned our young boys into thugs and our young girls into young whores."*

Kymo Dockett: You are revealing the truth about hip-hop. I would tell any young person that hip-hop by itself could be evil. Also, you are on point when you say that hip-hop, in general, is a culture that teaches our youth ungodly values. But every generation has had some kind of culture that was partially influenced by musical artists and ungodly values. Trust me, if hip-hop was not around, there would be another culture in place to negatively influence the youth. Therefore, you need to quit blaming hip-hop for the sinful condition of this generation and blame the Devil. I believe that Satan is using hip-hop to drag as many young people as he can to Hell. If this is true, why can't God use hip-hop for His purposes? Hip-hop is simply a tool, not the thing that is causing young people to go astray. The combination of words and notes put together is what makes music so powerful. When those words are nothing but death and lies, we must turn from it and not give it a place in our lives. However, when the words are words of Truth and Light, we are encouraged and empowered. What the Devil may mean for evil, God can use for much more good.

> "For we wrestle not against flesh and blood, but against principalities, against powers, against the rulers of the darkness of this world, against spiritual wickedness in high *places*." - **Eph. 6:12**

How do you know that the ministries who embrace Christian hip-hop did so because they were not being effective?

2. G. Craige Lewis said: *"There is a new move in our nation called Holy Hip-hop. It's a knock-off version of true Hip-hop but it is getting very popular among Youth Pastors and churches that do not effectively know how to reach the youth of their communities. Instead of fasting, praying, and seeking God for his Spirit to draw hearts that truly want to repent, they turn to Holy Hip-hop, which will speak the language, promote the look and appeal of the culture, and then add the message of Christ to it."*

Kymo Dockett: You claim that churches that don't effectively know how to reach the youth of their communities often turn to Holy Hip-hop. First of all, how do you know that the ministries who embrace Christian Hip-hop did so because they were not being effective? How do you know that these ministries don't fast, pray, and seek God for His Spirit to draw hearts that truly want to repent? Are you prepared to generate any evidence of this fact or is this simply a gross generalization?

Different Churches have embraced Christian hip-hop for various reasons. True, you don't need hip-hop to reach young people for Christ. Yet, many churches across the country have realized how effective and powerful Christian hip-hop has been. So why not use it? What evidence do you have that would indicate the Christian hip-hop is not impacting young people's lives for

Christ? This genre` has produced too much fruit for the Kingdom of God for someone to say it is not of God.

"A good tree cannot bring forth evil fruit; neither can a corrupt tree bring forth good fruit." – Mathew 7:17

Do you have to wear a three-piece suit to be a new creature in Christ?

3. G. Craige Lewis said: *"When I was not in Christ, I was a thief and a crook. Now that I am saved, am I a Holy Crook? Will these youth be transformed by the power of God and begin to look and act like NEW CREATURES? No, they will continue to live and look like the culture that had them spiritually bound in the first place. Ok, let's become a part of the pornographic culture to reach the pornographers. This is ridiculous. To reach the gothic culture or any other subculture, you must ask the real question. "Why are they Gothic?"*

Kymo Dockett: We have done more than slap the word 'holy' in front of hip-hop. Most catz within the Christian hip-hop community are just as on fire for God as Christians who don't participate in the hip-hop culture. We only dress and talk a little differently than the average Christian. The Bible mainly deals with the inner character you should have as a Christian. What is ungodly about wearing a ball cap or doo-rag? Are you attempting to say that, just because a person has on a pair of blue jeans and jersey, they can't be representin' Christ in their lifestyle? I personally have suggested that guys should always leave the house with a belt on, and that women should not wear any clothing that is sexually suggestive. Despite what you think, there is only a small minority of individuals involved in the Christian hip-hop community who may be mistaken for a thug or hoochie. Most look like your Average Joe.

Where in the Bible is there a dress code?

4. G. Craige Lewis said: *"I refuse to allow a man that looks thugged-out, gangstered-up, or a girl that is dressed "hoochie-fied" and whorish to get up* *and validate the Hip-hop lifestyle in my church. Many of our youth cannot get decent jobs or even finish school because they refuse to change their look for our society. They want to look gangster and thugged-out like the Hip-hop artists they see, but those artists are paid for looking like that, and our kids can't get ahead looking like them. Every school district I know of has rules against the many elements of Hip-Hop. They won't allow the music, the bandannas, the sagging, the "hoochie-mama outfits," doo-rags, jerseys, or hats. So is the church supposed to have lower standards than the public school?"*

Kymo Dockett: Christian hip-hop artists in general are not validating the hip-hop lifestyle. Have you ever seen a Christian hip-hop artist promote sex and violence to young people? Next time, please use specific examples of artists who are validating an ungodly lifestyle. And, please don't use **Kanye West**, because we do not claim him to be (nor does he claim to be) a Christian hip-hop artist. Can a person be dressed up in a three-piece suit and be wicked or evil? Why are you continually trying to draw a direct correlation between dress and lifestyles? Shouldn't we be judging artists on the fruit of their ministry and not whether they have a tie on? As long as that artist is being modest in his or her clothing, whether it be a jersey, t-shirt, or shirt and tie, we shouldn't be putting down the ministers or their ministries because of their clothing or dress-styles.

Also, why are you attempting to compare the church to a public school and their standards? Where in the Bible is there a dress code? Once again, I know that it is important to use common sense. No one should be dressed in church in a manner that will disrupt the flow of the service. For example, I can respect the fact that many churches still ask young men to remove their hats during service. But the fact that a person doesn't dress like the traditional church member doesn't mean these individuals are thugs or hoochies, or that they lack maturity as a Believer. That sounds like judgment. And we all need to be wary of judging others. The Sermon on the Mount reminds us that we shall be judged with the measure that we use, and to first take care of the plank in our own eyes before we bother with the specks in other peoples' eyes.

"For man looketh on the outward appearance, but the Lord looketh on the heart." – **1Samuel 16:7**

Just because I grant Shaq or Dwayne Wade props for being great basketball players, this doesn't mean I agree with what they stand for off the court.

5. G. Craige Lewis said: *"They want to give props to Hip-hop and bring this foul belief system into your church to validate the rebellion that already exists among your youth. They want to show your young boys that wearing big diamond earrings, "doo-rags", and baseball caps over wave caps is okay for church service. Did you ever notice that the Holy hip-hoppers always give "props" to Hip-hop not Holy Hip-hop? Even at some of their concerts, they have the youth chanting "Hip- Hop! Hip-hop!" Not "Holy hip-hop! Holy Hip-hop!" I guess "holy hip-hop" has too many syllables."*

Kymo Dockett: I believe that a church should only invite people to come minister if their ministries line up with the Word of God. This includes Christian emcees. If churches have any questions about the artist's beliefs, we encourage them to do the proper research on that particular artist. There is an immense difference between giving props and worshipping something. Just because I grant **Shaq** or **Dwayne Wade** props for being great basketball players, that doesn't mean I agree with what they stand for, off the court. I believe there is nothing wrong with respecting the artistic aspect of hip-hop, such as the skilled lyrics and well-crafted beats.

What I'm attempting to say is that there is nothing wrong with hip-hop itself, but the way this generation has decided to use it has been wrong. If someone decides to use traditional Gospel music in the wrong way, is there something wrong with traditional Gospel music or with the person who is using it? Let's stop wasting our time dealing with hip-hop as a genre. Instead, we should deal with the people who are using it to negatively influence our young people, not those who are encouraging and building up young people to follow Christ.

God will judge man by how we use what He creates.

6. G. Craige Lewis said: *"It must be understood that just because something is in existence does not mean that God created it and sanctions it. Child pornography exists, yet God didn't create it neither does he use it in any way. When we talk about music and culture we are talking about something that was manufactured using the raw materials and talents that God created. So, in that sense, sure God created everything. But many things that are manufactured by man, God does not want credited back to him."*

Kymo Dockett: God did create everything, but man is the one who misuses what God created. For example, God created sex to be enjoyed between a husband and wife. Man started to have sex outside the context of marriage, including getting involved in homosexual relationships and child pornography. Yet we still give credit to God for creating sex. God will judge man by how we use what He creates. It's the same with music. God is pleased when we utilize music for His purposes and will judge those who are using music for anything other than pleasing Him.

> "For by Him were all things created, that are in Heaven, and that are in Heaven, and that are in earth, visible and invisible, whether they be thrones, or powers: all things were created by Him, and for Him". – **Colossians 1:16**

It is silly to sit here and fight over doctrine issues while the world goes to Hell.

7. G. Craige Lewis said: *"Why call it Holy Hip-hop and not believe in the gifts of the Holy Ghost? The Holy Ghost will draw the sinner, but many Holy Hip-hop rappers deny the gifts and do not deal with the spirit realm concerning Hip-hop and the world. They don't cast out demons, they don't believe in divine healing, and many don't even believe in the baptism of the Holy Ghost!"*

Kymo Dockett: Here you go again with these sweeping statements. True, there are some artists within the Christian hip-hop community who don't believe in the gifts of the Holy Ghost.

These kinds of issues are only a reflection of diversity within the Body of Christ. Nowadays, almost every Church has a different doctrine. For example, some churches believe that women should not be allowed to preach; some churches think that women should wear prayer caps. I could go on, but I think you understand where I'm going. We must make sure the theology is right (God is holy; we are sinners; God sent His Son to earth as a human to die for our sins; and by accepting and following Christ, our sins are wiped clean and we will be with God in Heaven). The doctrinal issues are minor and should not continue to divide us; letting such issues divide us takes our focus off of saving the lost, and tears down our brothers and sisters.

Why are you grouping Kanye West with the Christian hip-hop community?

8. G. Craige Lewis said: *"Kanye West is packing out church altars when he makes his appeal for salvation, even though his music promotes sin, sex, and violence. How is he any different than a Holy Hip-hopper? They are both using Hip-hop to reach the youth, right? Effective youth ministries don't need gimmicks."*

Kymo Dockett: Kanye West is using hip-hop to make a living, and most Christian hip-hop artists are using Christian hip-hop to reach youth for Christ. Kanye West never professed to be a Christian hip-hop artist, nor does the Christian hip-hop community claim him. So why are you grouping him with the Christian hip-hop community? We were the ones who protested when the **Stellar Awards** tried to give him an award for Christian Hip-Hop Album of the Year. We did that because we didn't want our genre` to be associated with sin, sex, violence, and the other things Kanye promotes. Just because some churches may have tried to use Kanye as a ministry tool, don't assume that every Holy Hip-hop artist, promoter, or fan agreed with that decision.

What evidence is there that Christian hip-hop is a big push to make money?

9. G. Craige Lewis said: *"People of God understand that Holy Hip-hop is a ridiculous push to make money from the real Hip-hop!"*

Kymo Dockett: Last time I checked, there was no real money in Christian hip-hop. Most Christian hip-hop artists don't even make enough money to make a decent living. I don't know anyone who has gotten rich being a Christian hip-hop artist. Do you? If someone were looking to get rich, why would they go into something that has been around for over a decade that very few people have made any money off of? Again, these sweeping statements are based on biases and possibly a few examples. But please, don't put every Christian hip-hop artist in the same boat. Maybe you just haven't met the many genuine Christian hip-hop artists. I can introduce you to some, if you'd like.

So why are you picking on hip-hop? Why not go after Kirk Franklin, Fred Hammond and J. Moss?

10. G. Craige Lewis said: *"Da TRUTH says in one of his songs: "Hip-hop and the Gospel, a dynamic team!" Now we know that, if they are on the same team, that would make them similar. The word tells us, "How can 2 walk together, unless they agree?"*

Kymo Dockett: If two things are on the same team together, this means that they are together for a purpose. The particular Scripture you quoted is mostly talking about people joining themselves together. Hip-hop and the Gospel can be put on the same team with the purpose of leading young people to Christ. Then you would say, "Why not put stripping, weed smoking, and the Gospel together?". It is a Christian's responsibility to study the Word of God and examine what God will allow us to team with the Gospel to help lead souls to Him. Paul talked about changing the way he preached and what he said, according to the audience to which he was speaking. We're talking about the same thing. With the Truth of the Gospel as the foundation, we are changing the way we preach and how it is said, in order to reach another generation. It's the same message, but a different method.

Music and the Gospel have made a great team over the years. This is one reason why the Gospel music industry has grown. Hip-hop is only one form of music God is using to impact this generation, so why are you picking on hip-hop? Why not go after **Kirk Franklin, Fred Hammond** and **J. Moss**? Last time I checked, they were using music and the Gospel together, as well. I'm not proposing the opposition to spread to contemporary Gospel music. I just want to point out the fact that hip-hop is getting the bulk of the criticism, when R&B, rock, pop, and other styles of music are also being used in a negative fashion. God is still using groups like Out of Eden, Audio Adrenaline, and the Dave Crowder Band to make great strides for the Kingdom, even though they are R&B, rock, and pop styles of music.

REFERENCES AND NOTES

Introduction
Barna Research Group. *Twentysomethings Struggle to Find Their Place in Christian Churches*. Ventura: Barna Research Group, 2003.

Chapter 1
Barna Research Group. *Parents Describe How They Raise Their Children*. Ventura: Barna Research Group, February 28, 2005.

Becker, Eddie. *Chronology on the History of Slavery*. Washington, DC: Office of Architectural History, 1999.

Bositis, David. *Black Elected Officials: A Statistical Summary*. Washington, D. C.: Joint Center Publications, 2001.

Encyclop–dia Britannica Premium. "National Baptist Convention of the United States of America,

Inc." Illinois: *Encyclop–dia Britannica*, 2005.

Kitwana, Bakari. *The Hip Hop Generation: Young Blacks and the Crisis in African-American Culture*. New York: Basic Cerivtas Books, 2002.

Sutton, Charyn D. *Pass It On: Outreach to Minority Communities*. Philadelphia: Energize, Inc., 2005.

Chapter 2
Shapiro, Jeffrey. "Letter: Reject Farrakhan." *The Daily Illini*, October 27, 2004.

Sutton, Charyn D. *Pass It On: Outreach to Minority Communities*. Philadelphia: Energize, Inc., 2005.

Chapter 3
BigNewsNetwork.com. Research study of popularity of hip-hop and rap music among teens. Edison Media Research, October 20, 2004.

Gray-Kontar, Daniel. "Does hip-hop music help or hurt students' attitudes toward education?" *The Community Renewal Society*, April 2005.

Kitwana, Bakari. *The Hip Hop Generation: Young Blacks and the Crisis in African-American Culture.* New York: Basic Cerivtas Books, 2002.

Light, Alan. *The Vibe History of Hip Hop.* New York: Three Rivers Press, 1999.

Chapter 4

Clark, Chap. *Hurt.* Grand Rapids: Baker Academic Press, 2004.

DeVries, Mark. *Family-Based Youth Ministry.* Downers Grove: InterVarsity Press, 1994.

McIntosh, Gary L. *One Church, Four Generations.* Grand Rapids: Baker Books, 2002.

Chapter 5

Note: Information collected for Christian Hip Hop 101 came from various Web sites, including www.rapzilla.com, www.holycultureradio.com, www.sphereofhiphop.com and www.wtwmagazine.com.

Bonus Section #1

Note: Information collected for the History of Christian Hip-Hop came from a series of interviews and Web sites, including www.artistdirect.com, www.crossrhythms.co.uk, www.musiq.pl, mp3.com, www.ccmmagazine.com and www.christianitytoday.com.

Printed in the United States
42743LVS00002B/94-279